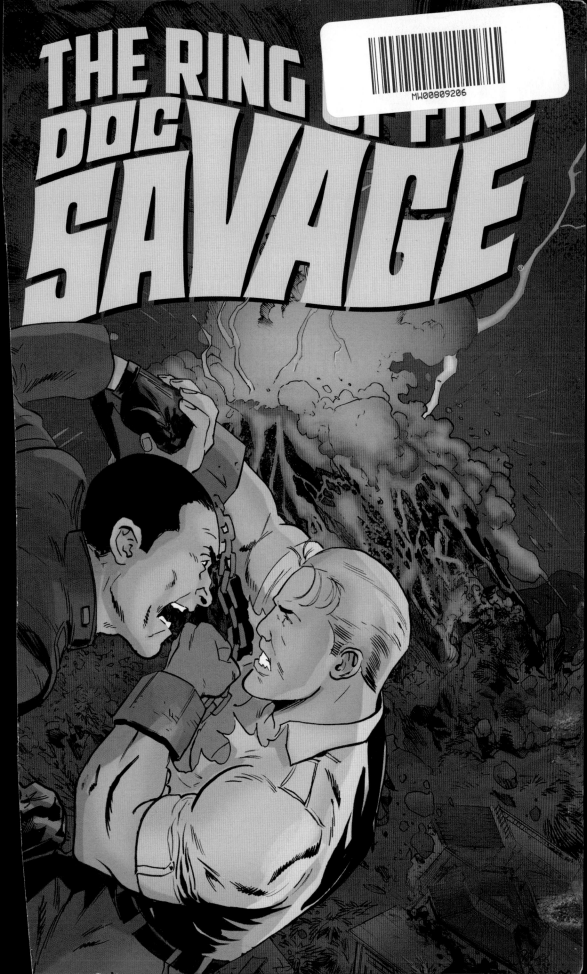

THE RING OF FIRE

DOC SAVAGE

WRITTEN BY
DAVID AVALLONE

ART BY
DAVE ACOSTA

COLORS BY
MORGAN HICKMAN AND REBECCA NALTY

LETTERS BY
TAYLOR ESPOSITO

COVER BY
BRENT SCHOONOVER

COLLECTION DESIGN BY
GEOFF HARKINS

EDITED BY
ANTHONY MARQUES

Nick Barrucci, CEO / Publisher
Juan Collado, President / COO

Joe Rybandt, Executive Editor
Matt Idelson, Senior Editor
Anthony Marques, Associate Editor
Matt Humphreys, Assistant Editor
Kevin Ketner, Assistant Editor

Jason Ullmeyer, Art Director
Geoff Harkins, Senior Graphic Designer
Cathleen Heard, Graphic Designer
Alexis Persson, Graphic Designer

Chris Caniano, Digital Associate
Rachel Kilbury, Digital Assistant

Brandon Dante Primavera, V.P. of IT and Operations
Rich Young, Director of Business Development

Online at www.DYNAMITE.com
On Facebook /Dynamitecomics
On Instagram /Dynamitecomics

Alan Payne, V.P. of Sales and Marketing
Keith Davidsen, Marketing Director
Pat O'Connell, Sales Manager

On Tumblr dynamitecomics.tumblr.com
On Twitter @dynamitecomics
On YouTube /Dynamitecomics

First Printing   ISBN-13: 978-1-5241-0446-7   10 9 8 7 6 5 4 3 2 1

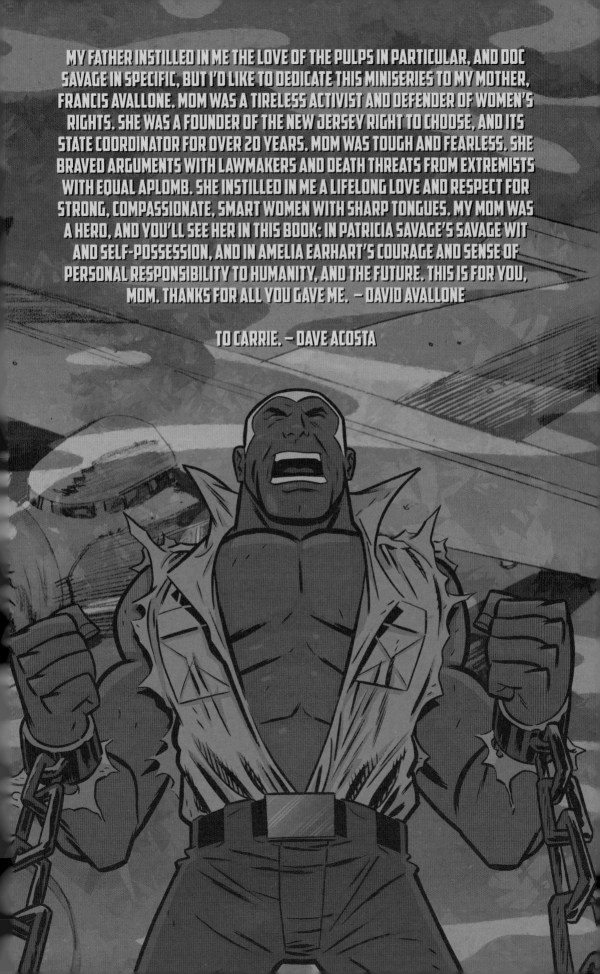

MY FATHER INSTILLED IN ME THE LOVE OF THE PULPS IN PARTICULAR, AND DOC SAVAGE IN SPECIFIC, BUT I'D LIKE TO DEDICATE THIS MINISERIES TO MY MOTHER, FRANCIS AVALLONE. MOM WAS A TIRELESS ACTIVIST AND DEFENDER OF WOMEN'S RIGHTS. SHE WAS A FOUNDER OF THE NEW JERSEY RIGHT TO CHOOSE, AND ITS STATE COORDINATOR FOR OVER 20 YEARS. MOM WAS TOUGH AND FEARLESS. SHE BRAVED ARGUMENTS WITH LAWMAKERS AND DEATH THREATS FROM EXTREMISTS WITH EQUAL APLOMB. SHE INSTILLED IN ME A LIFELONG LOVE AND RESPECT FOR STRONG, COMPASSIONATE, SMART WOMEN WITH SHARP TONGUES. MY MOM WAS A HERO, AND YOU'LL SEE HER IN THIS BOOK: IN PATRICIA SAVAGE'S SAVAGE WIT AND SELF-POSSESSION, AND IN AMELIA EARHART'S COURAGE AND SENSE OF PERSONAL RESPONSIBILITY TO HUMANITY, AND THE FUTURE. THIS IS FOR YOU, MOM. THANKS FOR ALL YOU GAVE ME. — DAVID AVALLONE

TO CARRIE. — DAVE ACOSTA

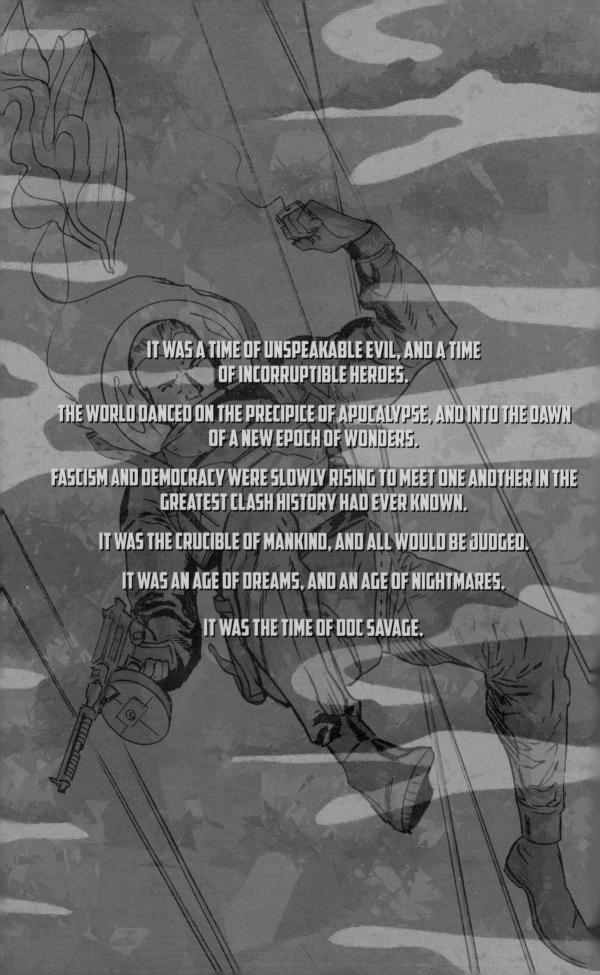

IT WAS A TIME OF UNSPEAKABLE EVIL, AND A TIME
OF INCORRUPTIBLE HEROES.

THE WORLD DANCED ON THE PRECIPICE OF APOCALYPSE, AND INTO THE DAWN
OF A NEW EPOCH OF WONDERS.

FASCISM AND DEMOCRACY WERE SLOWLY RISING TO MEET ONE ANOTHER IN THE
GREATEST CLASH HISTORY HAD EVER KNOWN.

IT WAS THE CRUCIBLE OF MANKIND, AND ALL WOULD BE JUDGED.

IT WAS AN AGE OF DREAMS, AND AN AGE OF NIGHTMARES.

IT WAS THE TIME OF DOC SAVAGE.

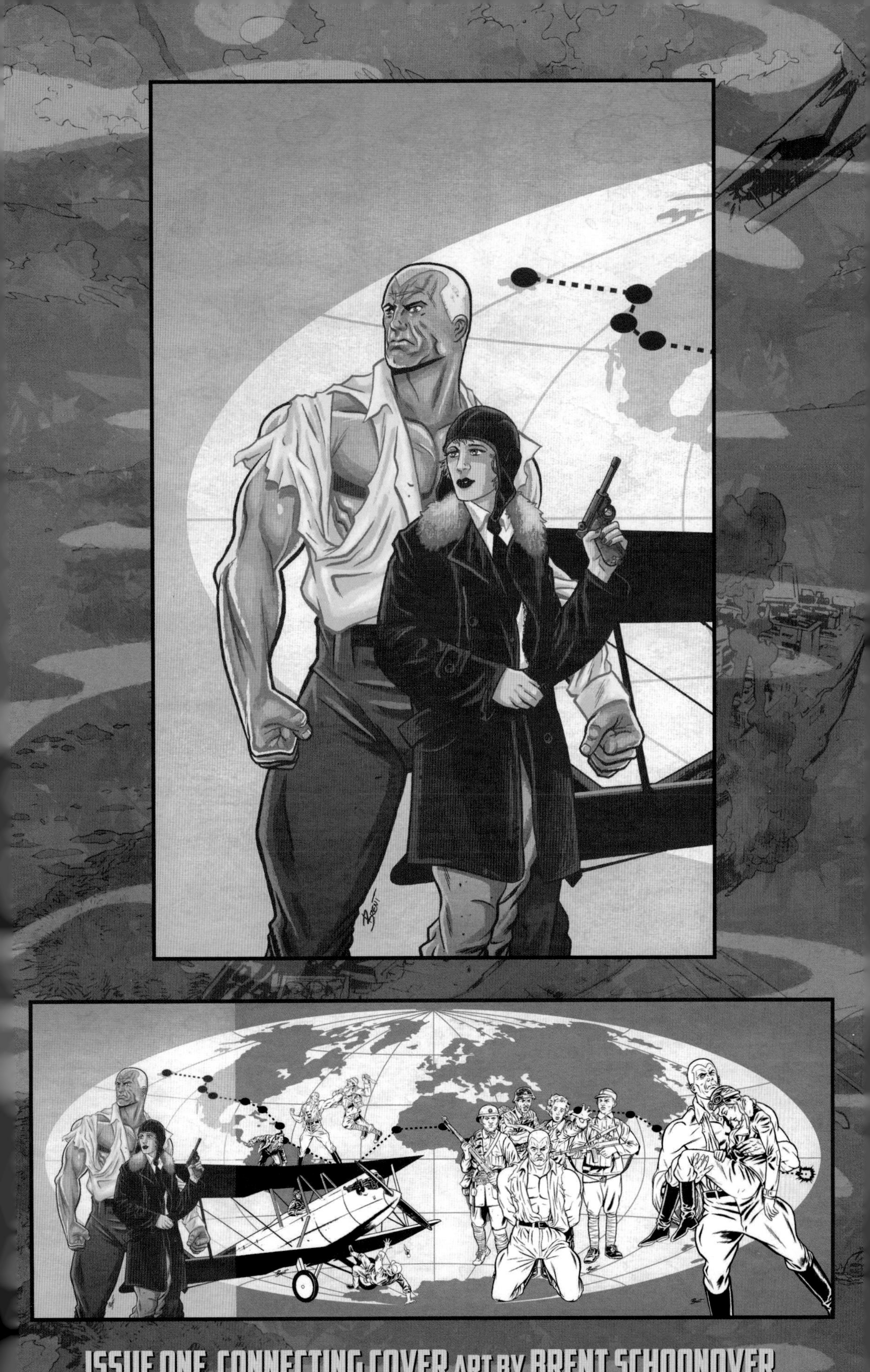

ISSUE ONE CONNECTING COVER ART BY BRENT SCHOONOVER

ONE

"FIREBIRD"

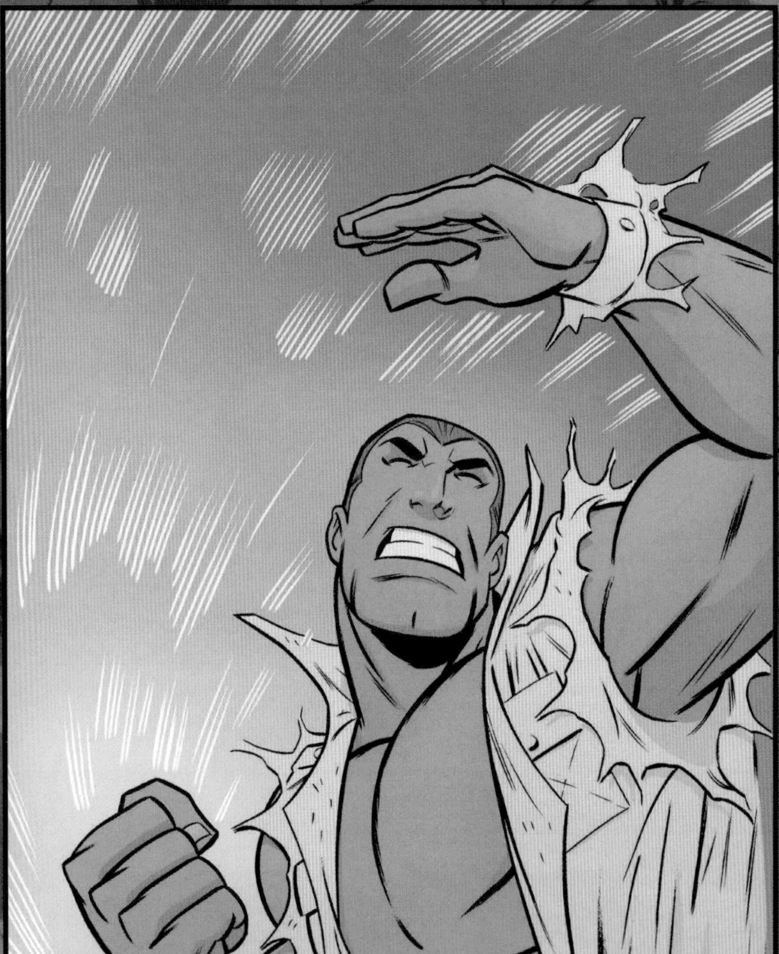
MARQUES
J.BONE
2016

ISSUE ONE VARIANT COVER ART BY ANTHONY MARQUES
INKS BY J. BONE, COLORS BY DANIELA MIWA

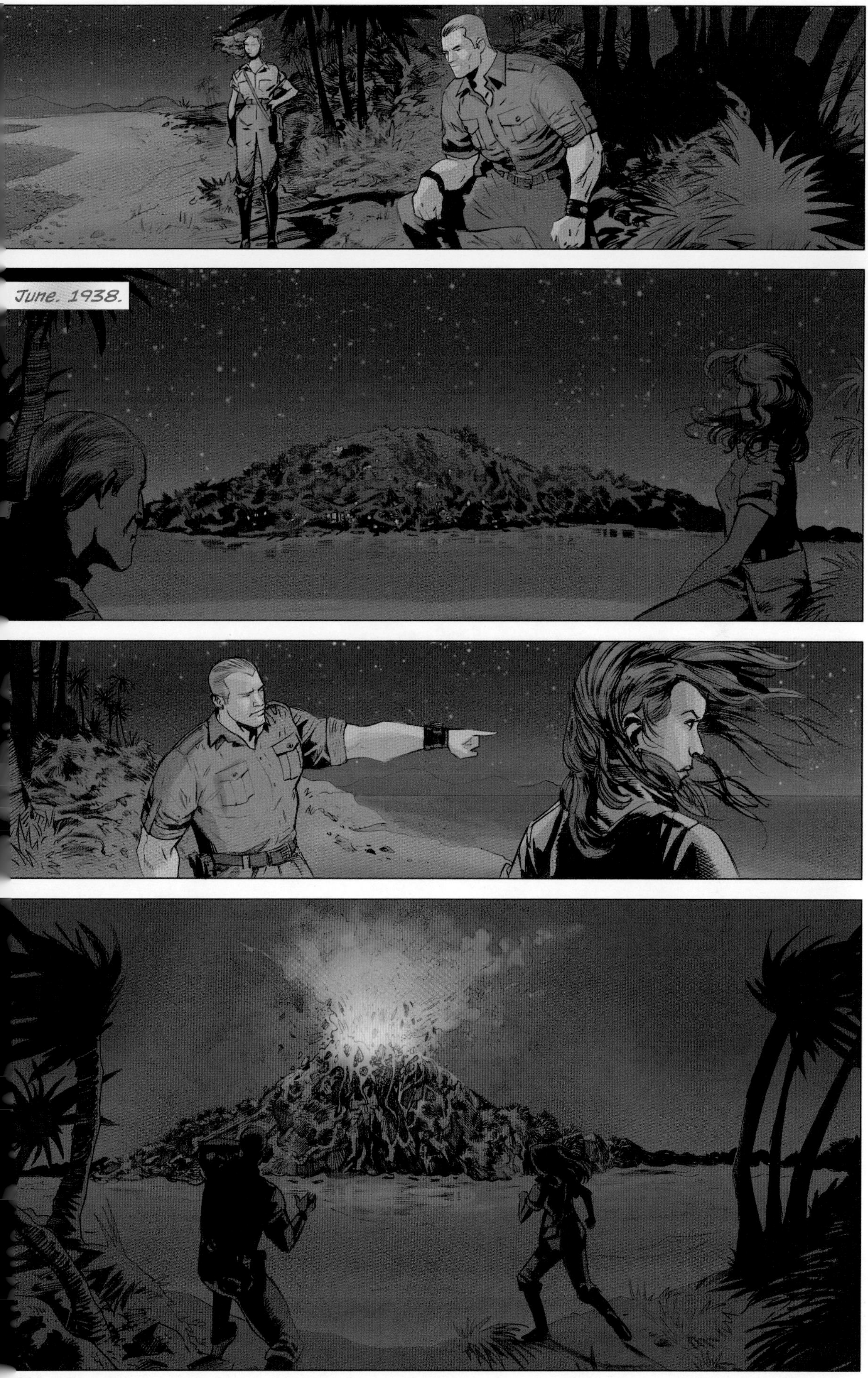
June. 1938.

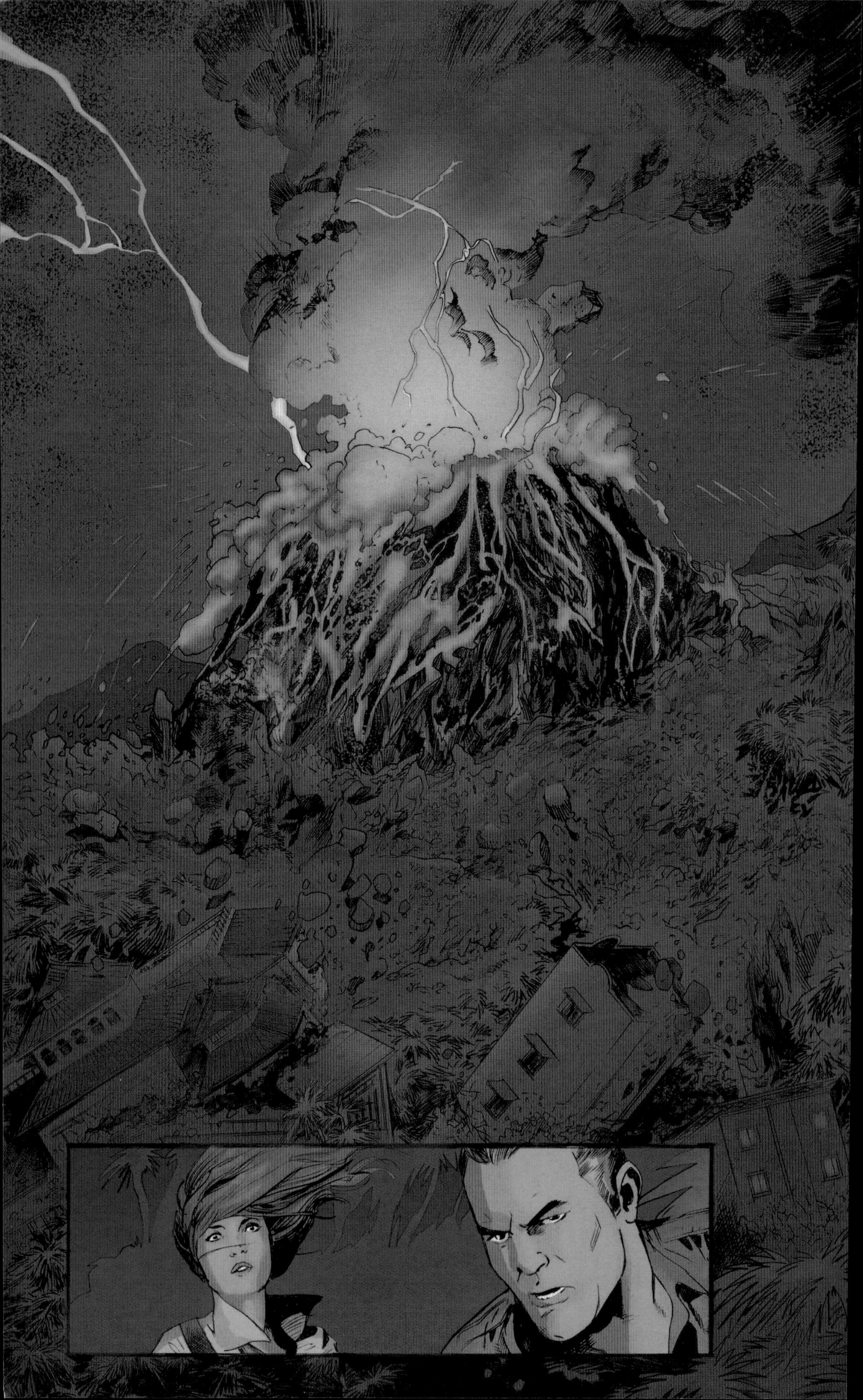

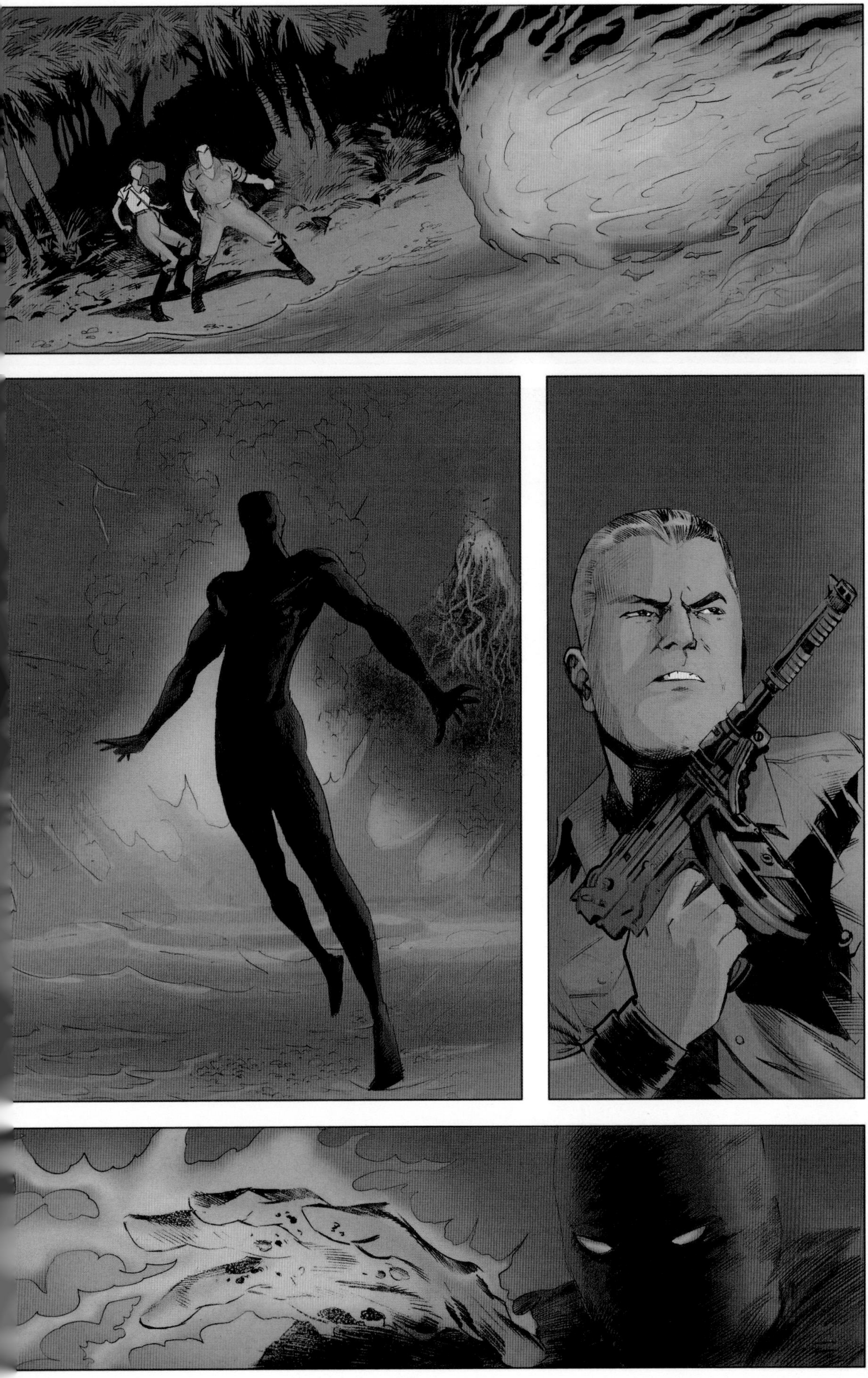

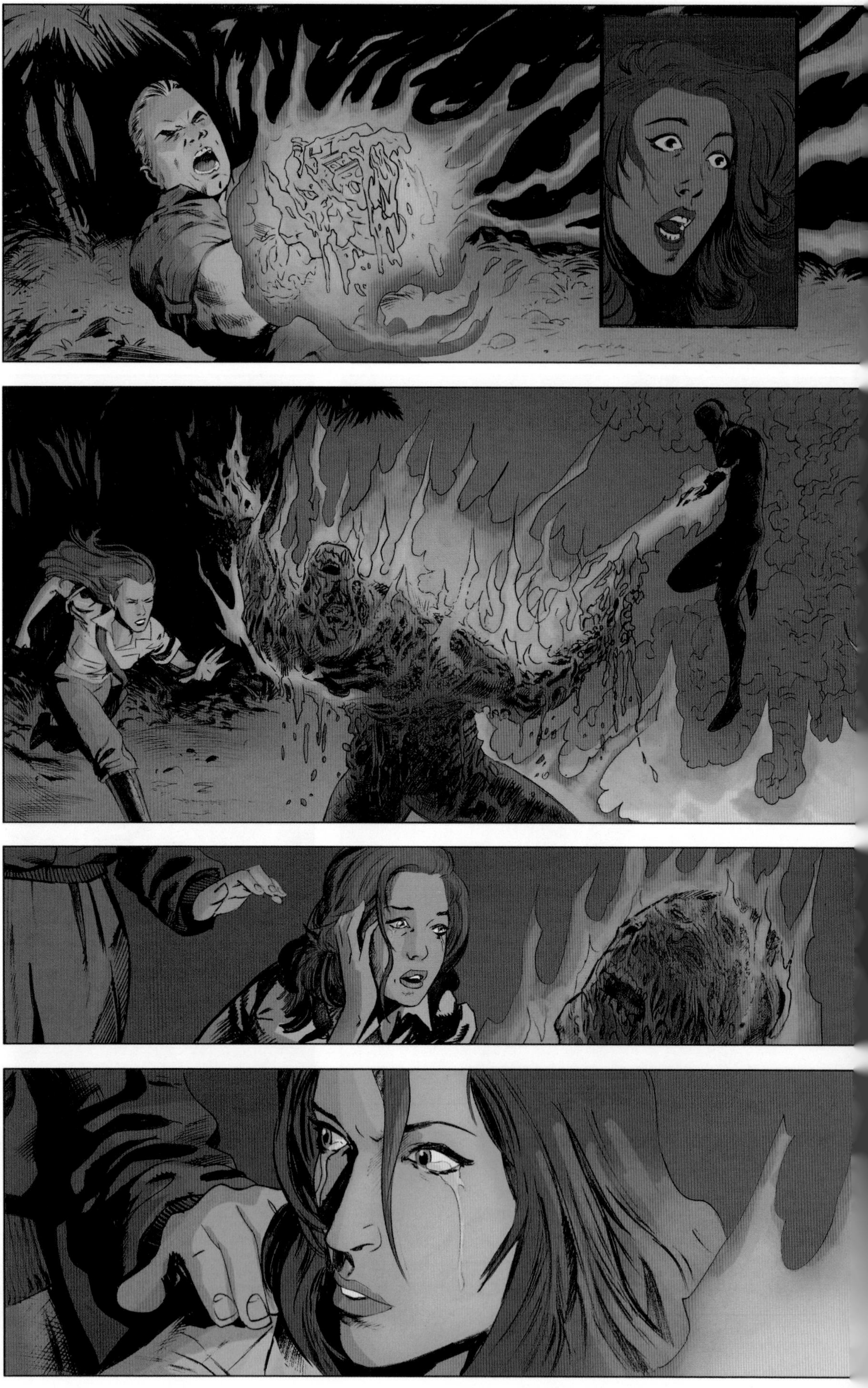

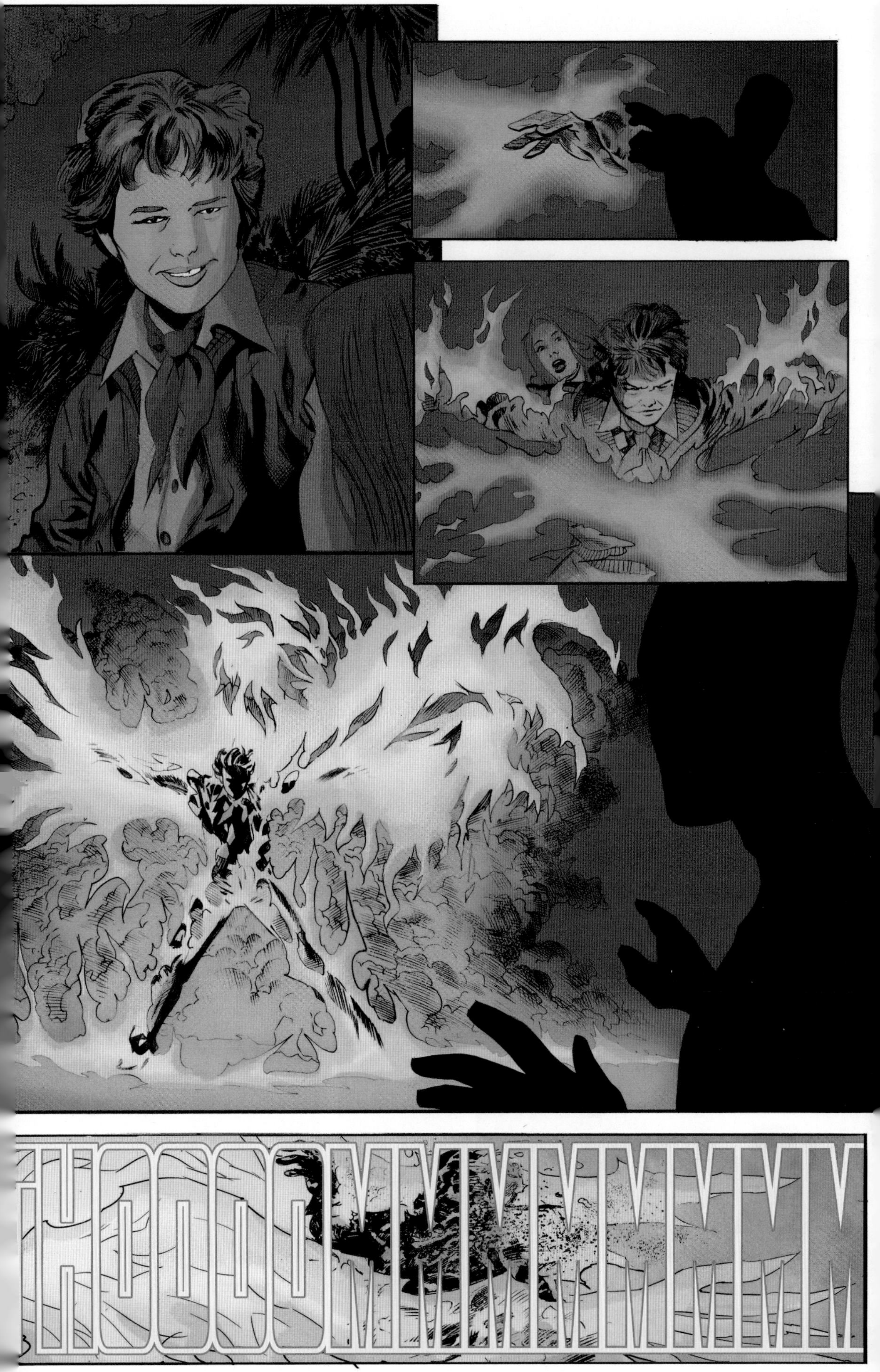
THOOOOMMMMMMMM

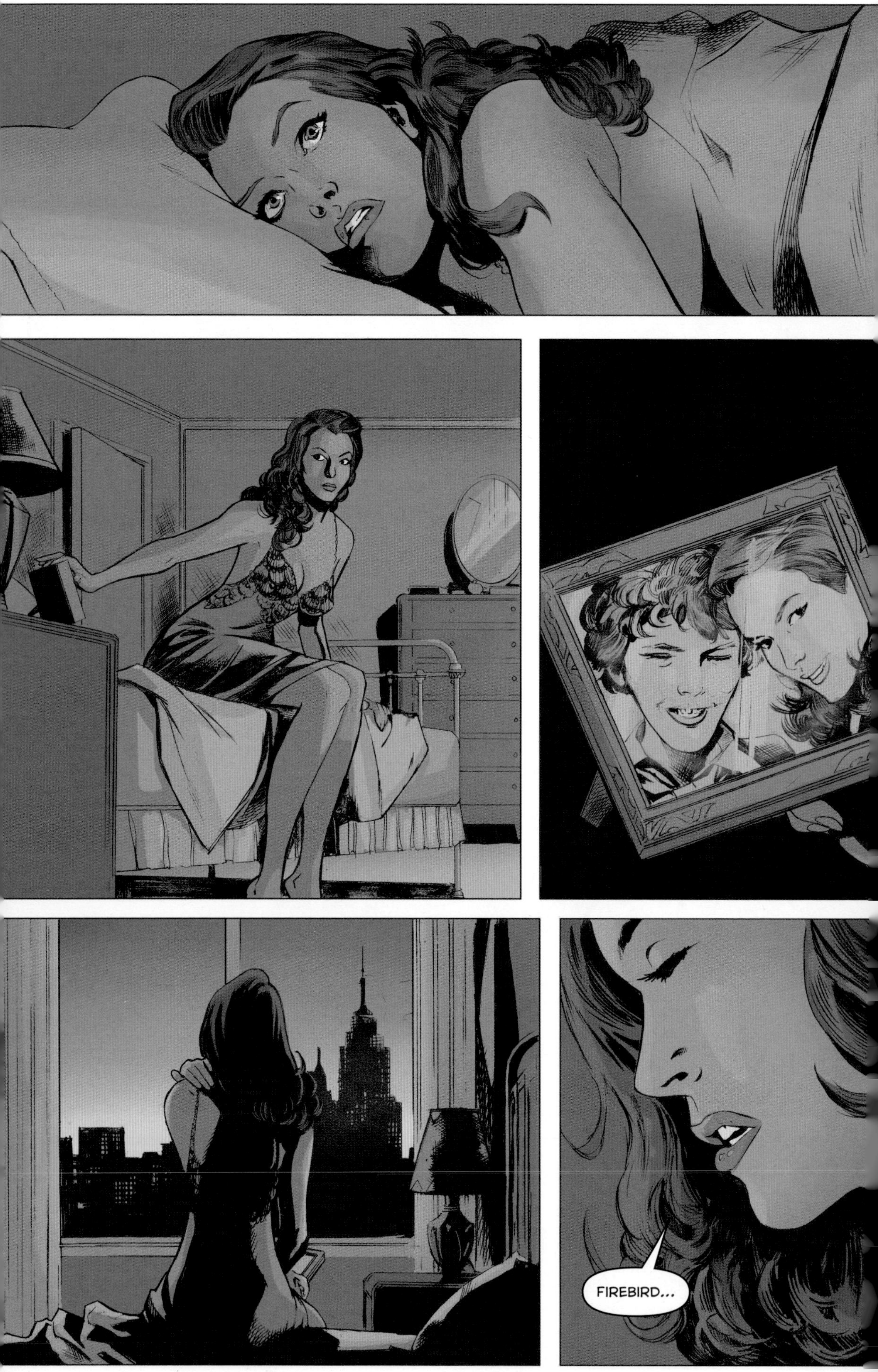
FIREBIRD...

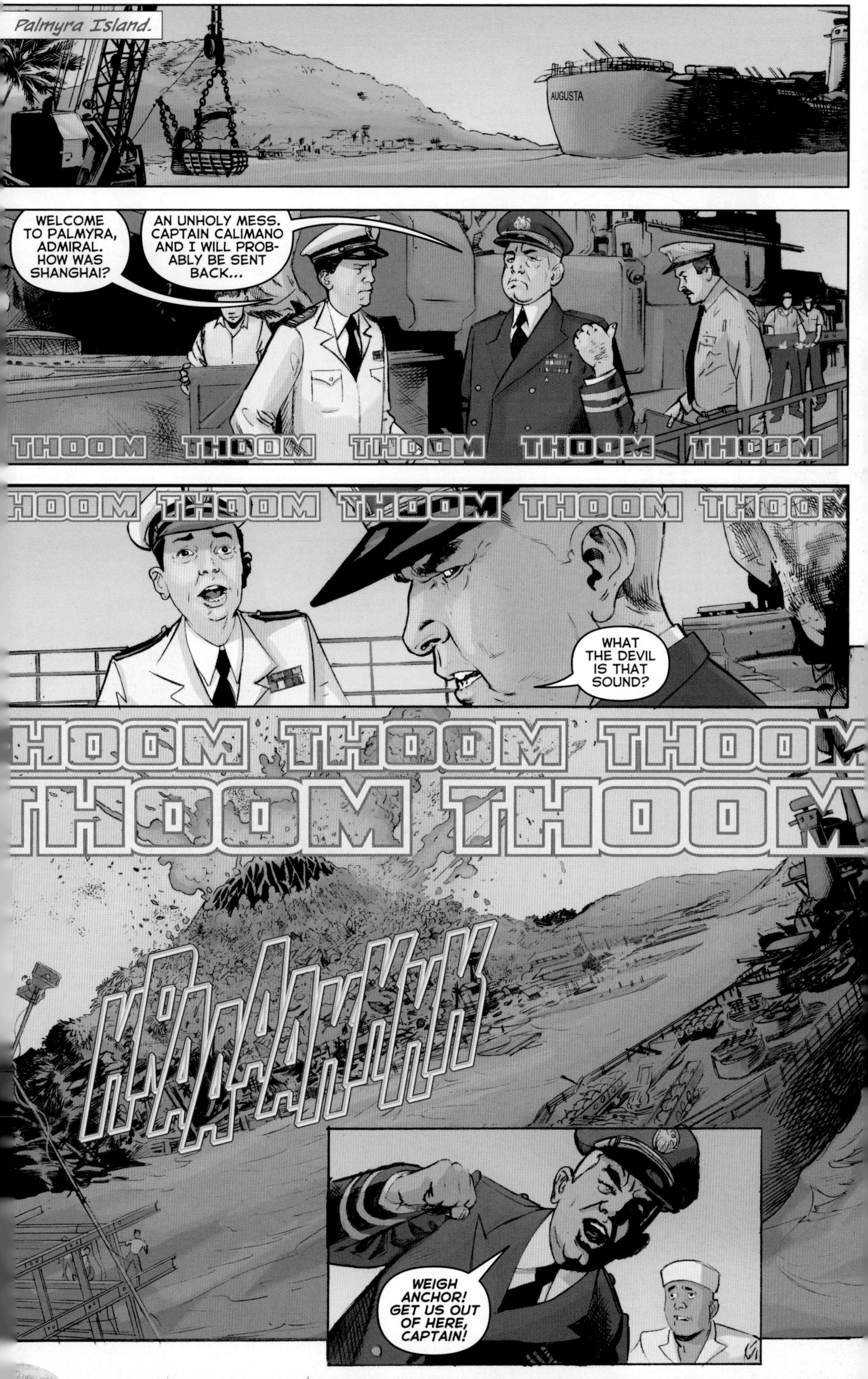
Palmyra Island.
AUGUSTA
WELCOME TO PALMYRA, ADMIRAL. HOW WAS SHANGHAI?
AN UNHOLY MESS. CAPTAIN CALIMANO AND I WILL PROBABLY BE SENT BACK...
THOOM THOOM THOOM THOOM THOOM
THOOM THOOM THOOM THOOM THOOM
WHAT THE DEVIL IS THAT SOUND?
THOOM THOOM THOOM
THOOM THOOM
WEIGH ANCHOR! GET US OUT OF HERE, CAPTAIN!

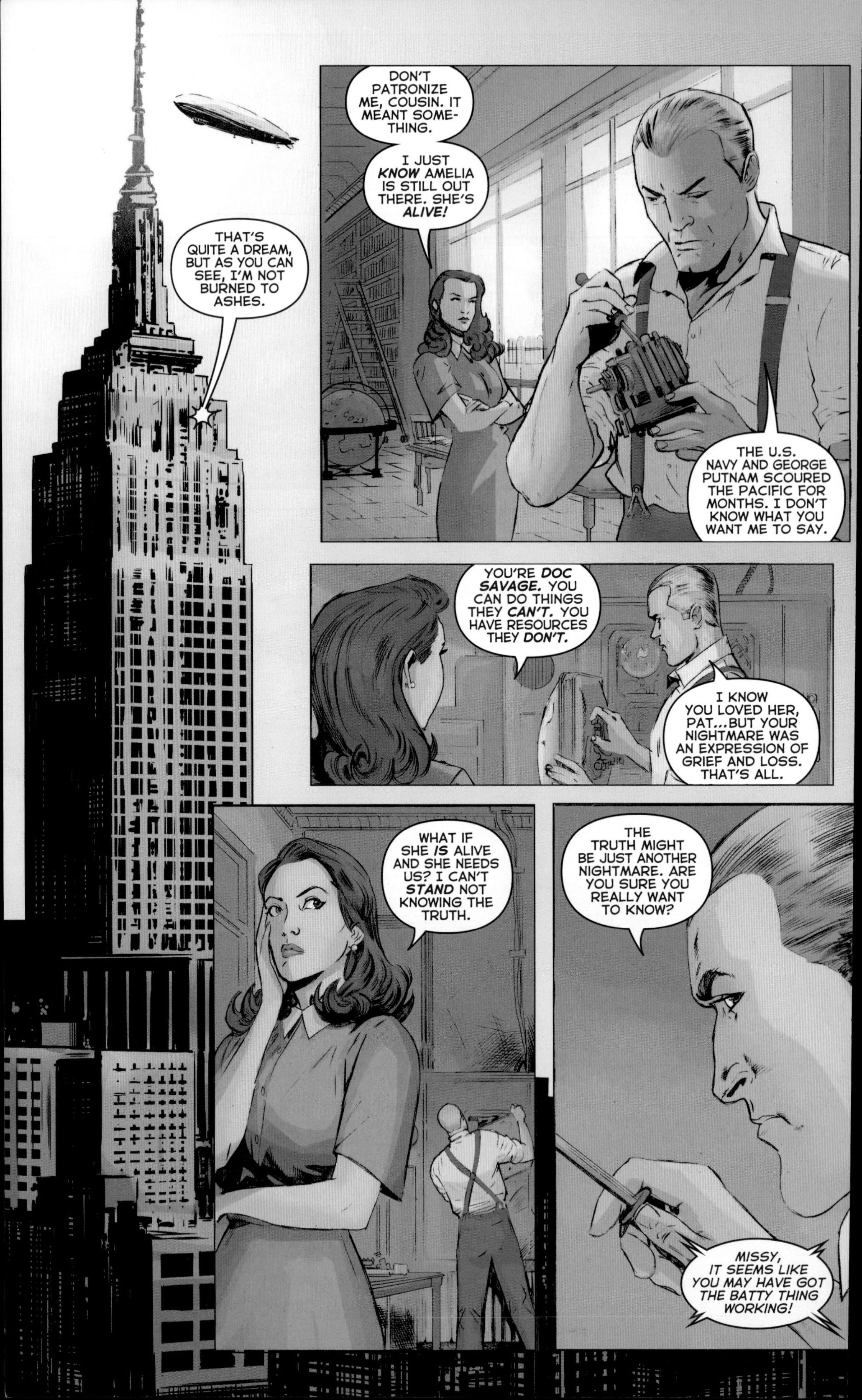
THAT'S QUITE A DREAM, BUT AS YOU CAN SEE, I'M NOT BURNED TO ASHES.
DON'T PATRONIZE ME, COUSIN. IT MEANT SOME-THING.
I JUST KNOW AMELIA IS STILL OUT THERE. SHE'S ALIVE!
THE U.S. NAVY AND GEORGE PUTNAM SCOURED THE PACIFIC FOR MONTHS. I DON'T KNOW WHAT YOU WANT ME TO SAY.
YOU'RE DOC SAVAGE. YOU CAN DO THINGS THEY CAN'T. YOU HAVE RESOURCES THEY DON'T.
I KNOW YOU LOVED HER, PAT...BUT YOUR NIGHTMARE WAS AN EXPRESSION OF GRIEF AND LOSS. THAT'S ALL.
WHAT IF SHE IS ALIVE AND SHE NEEDS US? I CAN'T STAND NOT KNOWING THE TRUTH.
THE TRUTH MIGHT BE JUST ANOTHER NIGHTMARE. ARE YOU SURE YOU REALLY WANT TO KNOW?
MISSY, IT SEEMS LIKE YOU MAY HAVE GOT THE BATTY THING WORKING!

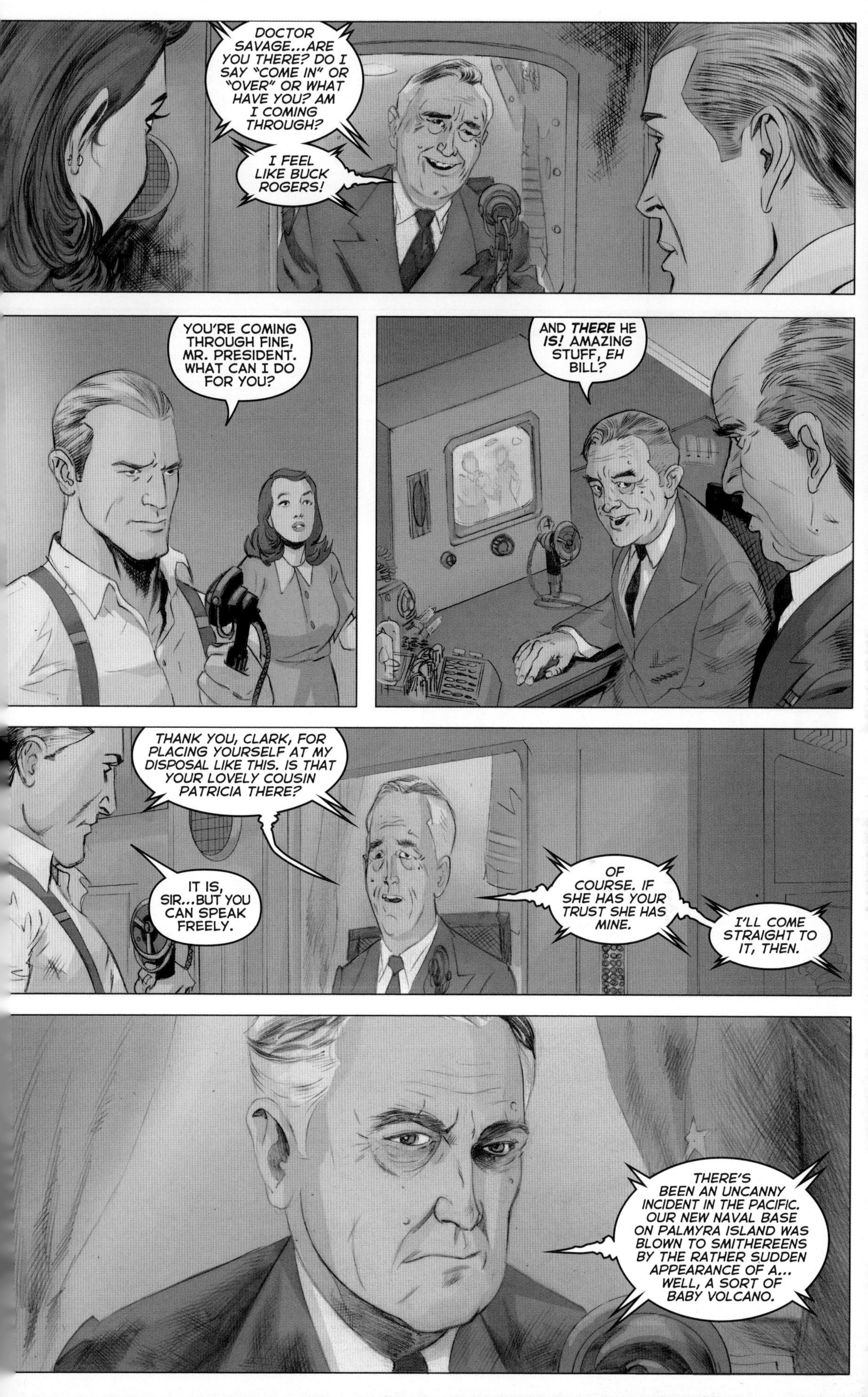
DOCTOR SAVAGE...ARE YOU THERE? DO I SAY "COME IN" OR "OVER" OR WHAT HAVE YOU? AM I COMING THROUGH?
I FEEL LIKE BUCK ROGERS!
YOU'RE COMING THROUGH FINE, MR. PRESIDENT. WHAT CAN I DO FOR YOU?
AND THERE HE IS! AMAZING STUFF, EH BILL?
THANK YOU, CLARK, FOR PLACING YOURSELF AT MY DISPOSAL LIKE THIS. IS THAT YOUR LOVELY COUSIN PATRICIA THERE?
IT IS, SIR...BUT YOU CAN SPEAK FREELY.
OF COURSE. IF SHE HAS YOUR TRUST SHE HAS MINE.
I'LL COME STRAIGHT TO IT, THEN.
THERE'S BEEN AN UNCANNY INCIDENT IN THE PACIFIC. OUR NEW NAVAL BASE ON PALMYRA ISLAND WAS BLOWN TO SMITHEREENS BY THE RATHER SUDDEN APPEARANCE OF A... WELL, A SORT OF BABY VOLCANO.

I'M NO GEOLOGIST, BUT EVEN I KNOW A VOLCANO, SUDDENLY APPEARING IN THE PACIFIC...IN AND OF ITSELF, IS NOT SUCH A SURPRISING THING.

BUT THERE ARE THREE DETAILS WHICH CAUSE MY SUSPICIOUS OLD MIND SOME ALARM...

ONE: THE NAVY BOYS TELL US THEY HEARD A MECHANICAL DRONING SOUND BEFORE THE ERUPTION.

TWO: PALMYRA ISLAND WAS SURVEYED JUST TWO MONTHS AGO AND THE REPORT CAME BACK 100% STABLE.

THREE: WITH ALL THE VAST PACIFIC OCEAN TO CHOOSE FROM, THIS LITTLE VOLCANO DECIDED TO POP UP UNDER OUR NEWEST NAVAL BASE, AND A FEW HUNDRED YARDS FROM THE HEAVY CRUISER U.S.S. AUGUSTA.

I SEE. WAS THE COMMANDER IN CHIEF OF THE ASIATIC FLEET ABOARD HER?

YES, ADMIRAL YARNELL WAS THERE. AUGUSTA GOT OUT A DISTRESS MESSAGE ABOUT THE VOLCANO, BUT A FEW MINUTES LATER WENT OFF THE AIR.

SO YOU SEE MY CONCERN? ANY-THING IS POSSIBLE, AND IT COULD ALL BE A COINCIDENCE...

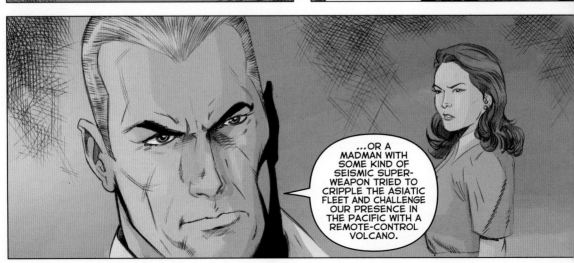

...OR A MADMAN WITH SOME KIND OF SEISMIC SUPER-WEAPON TRIED TO CRIPPLE THE ASIATIC FLEET AND CHALLENGE OUR PRESENCE IN THE PACIFIC WITH A REMOTE-CONTROL VOLCANO.

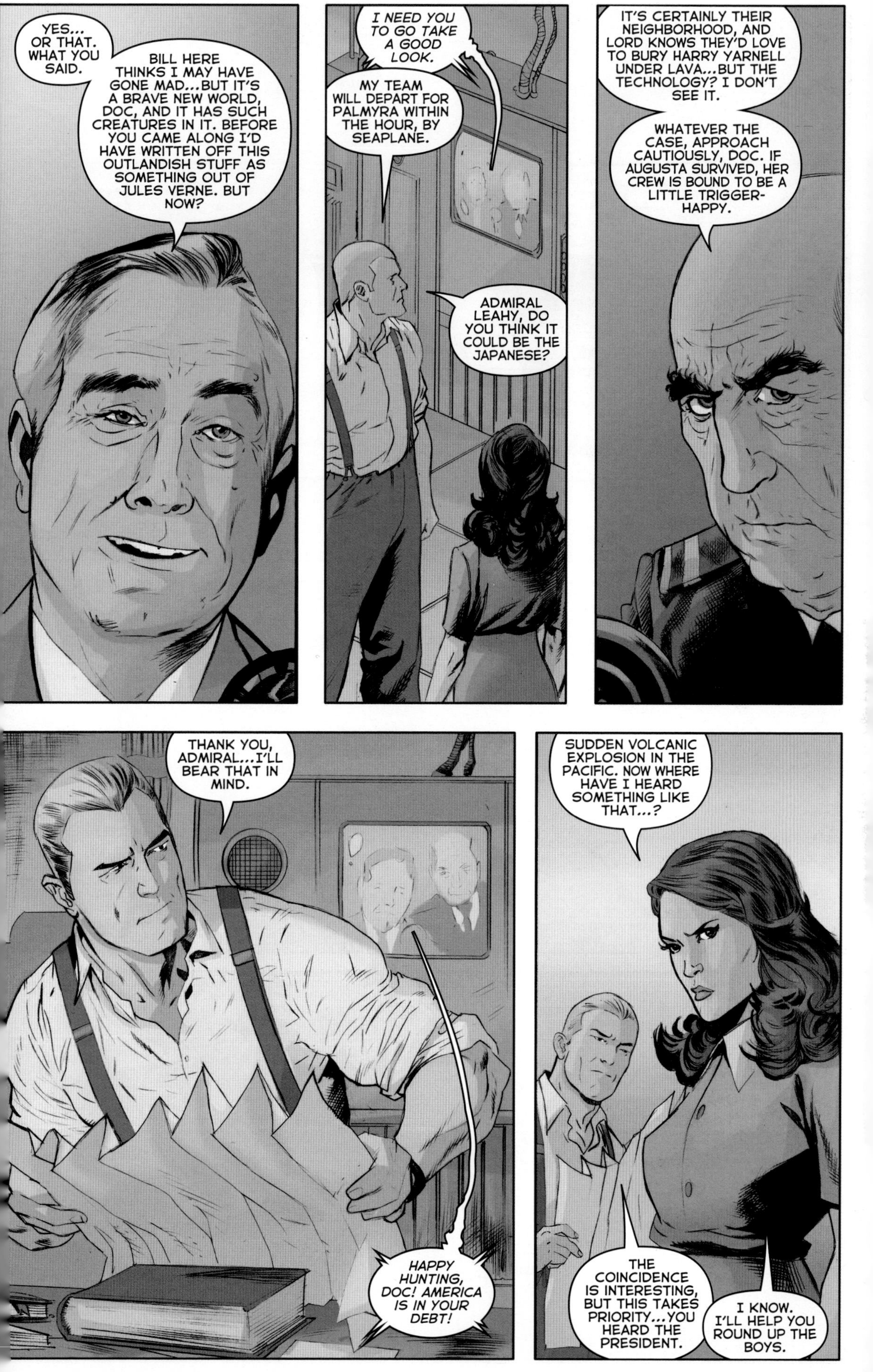
YES... OR THAT. WHAT YOU SAID.
BILL HERE THINKS I MAY HAVE GONE MAD...BUT IT'S A BRAVE NEW WORLD, DOC, AND IT HAS SUCH CREATURES IN IT. BEFORE YOU CAME ALONG I'D HAVE WRITTEN OFF THIS OUTLANDISH STUFF AS SOMETHING OUT OF JULES VERNE. BUT NOW?
I NEED YOU TO GO TAKE A GOOD LOOK.
MY TEAM WILL DEPART FOR PALMYRA WITHIN THE HOUR, BY SEAPLANE.
ADMIRAL LEAHY, DO YOU THINK IT COULD BE THE JAPANESE?
IT'S CERTAINLY THEIR NEIGHBORHOOD, AND LORD KNOWS THEY'D LOVE TO BURY HARRY YARNELL UNDER LAVA...BUT THE TECHNOLOGY? I DON'T SEE IT.
WHATEVER THE CASE, APPROACH CAUTIOUSLY, DOC. IF AUGUSTA SURVIVED, HER CREW IS BOUND TO BE A LITTLE TRIGGER-HAPPY.
THANK YOU, ADMIRAL...I'LL BEAR THAT IN MIND.
HAPPY HUNTING, DOC! AMERICA IS IN YOUR DEBT!
SUDDEN VOLCANIC EXPLOSION IN THE PACIFIC. NOW WHERE HAVE I HEARD SOMETHING LIKE THAT...?
THE COINCIDENCE IS INTERESTING, BUT THIS TAKES PRIORITY...YOU HEARD THE PRESIDENT.
I KNOW. I'LL HELP YOU ROUND UP THE BOYS.

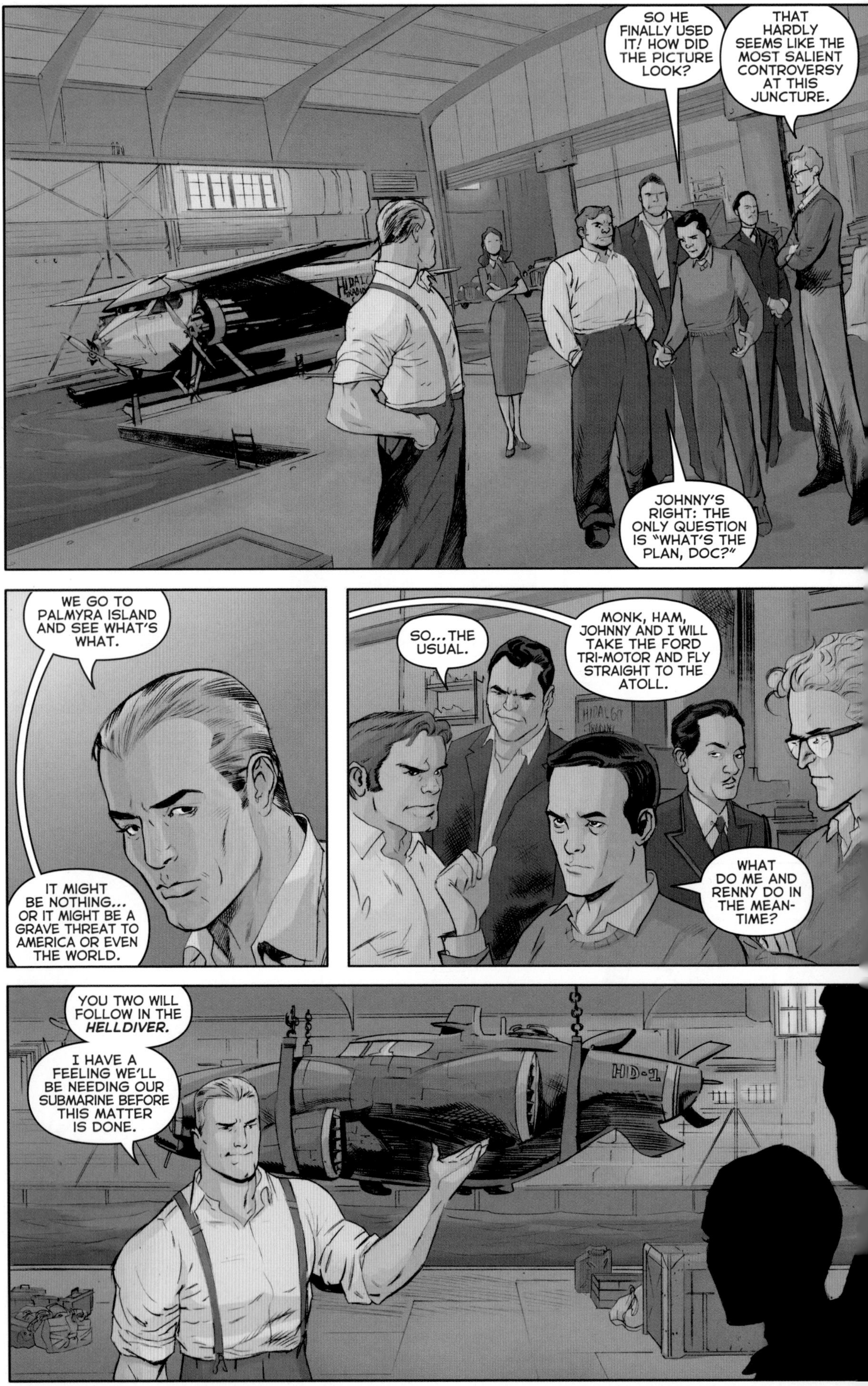
SO HE FINALLY USED IT! HOW DID THE PICTURE LOOK?
THAT HARDLY SEEMS LIKE THE MOST SALIENT CONTROVERSY AT THIS JUNCTURE.
JOHNNY'S RIGHT: THE ONLY QUESTION IS "WHAT'S THE PLAN, DOC?"
WE GO TO PALMYRA ISLAND AND SEE WHAT'S WHAT.
IT MIGHT BE NOTHING... OR IT MIGHT BE A GRAVE THREAT TO AMERICA OR EVEN THE WORLD.
MONK, HAM, JOHNNY AND I WILL TAKE THE FORD TRI-MOTOR AND FLY STRAIGHT TO THE ATOLL.
SO...THE USUAL.
WHAT DO ME AND RENNY DO IN THE MEAN-TIME?
YOU TWO WILL FOLLOW IN THE ***HELLDIVER.***
I HAVE A FEELING WE'LL BE NEEDING OUR SUBMARINE BEFORE THIS MATTER IS DONE.
HD-1

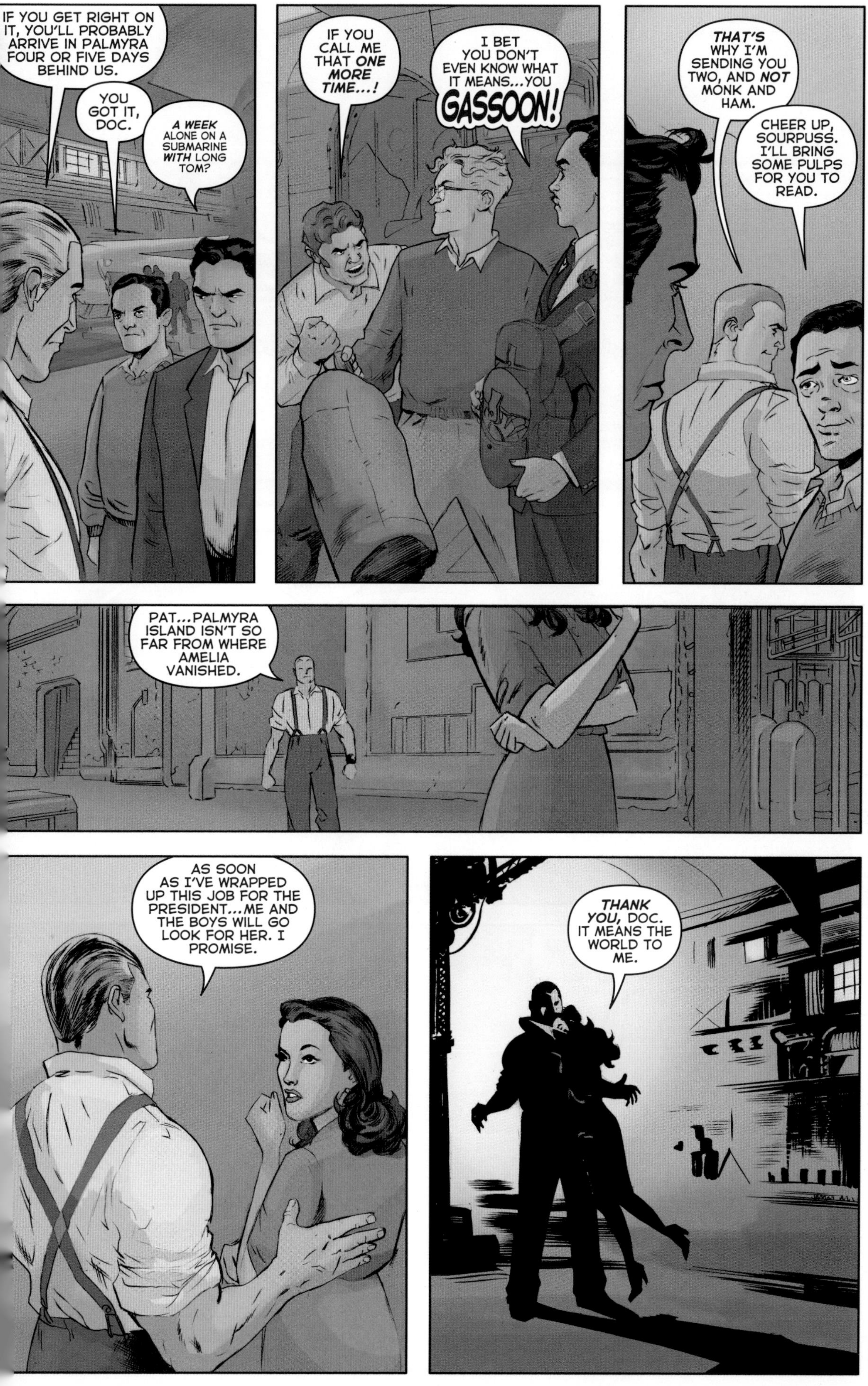
IF YOU GET RIGHT ON IT, YOU'LL PROBABLY ARRIVE IN PALMYRA FOUR OR FIVE DAYS BEHIND US.
YOU GOT IT, DOC.
A WEEK ALONE ON A SUBMARINE WITH LONG TOM?
IF YOU CALL ME THAT ONE MORE TIME...!
I BET YOU DON'T EVEN KNOW WHAT IT MEANS...YOU GASSOON!
THAT'S WHY I'M SENDING YOU TWO, AND NOT MONK AND HAM.
CHEER UP, SOURPUSS. I'LL BRING SOME PULPS FOR YOU TO READ.
PAT...PALMYRA ISLAND ISN'T SO FAR FROM WHERE AMELIA VANISHED.
AS SOON AS I'VE WRAPPED UP THIS JOB FOR THE PRESIDENT...ME AND THE BOYS WILL GO LOOK FOR HER. I PROMISE.
THANK YOU, DOC. IT MEANS THE WORLD TO ME.

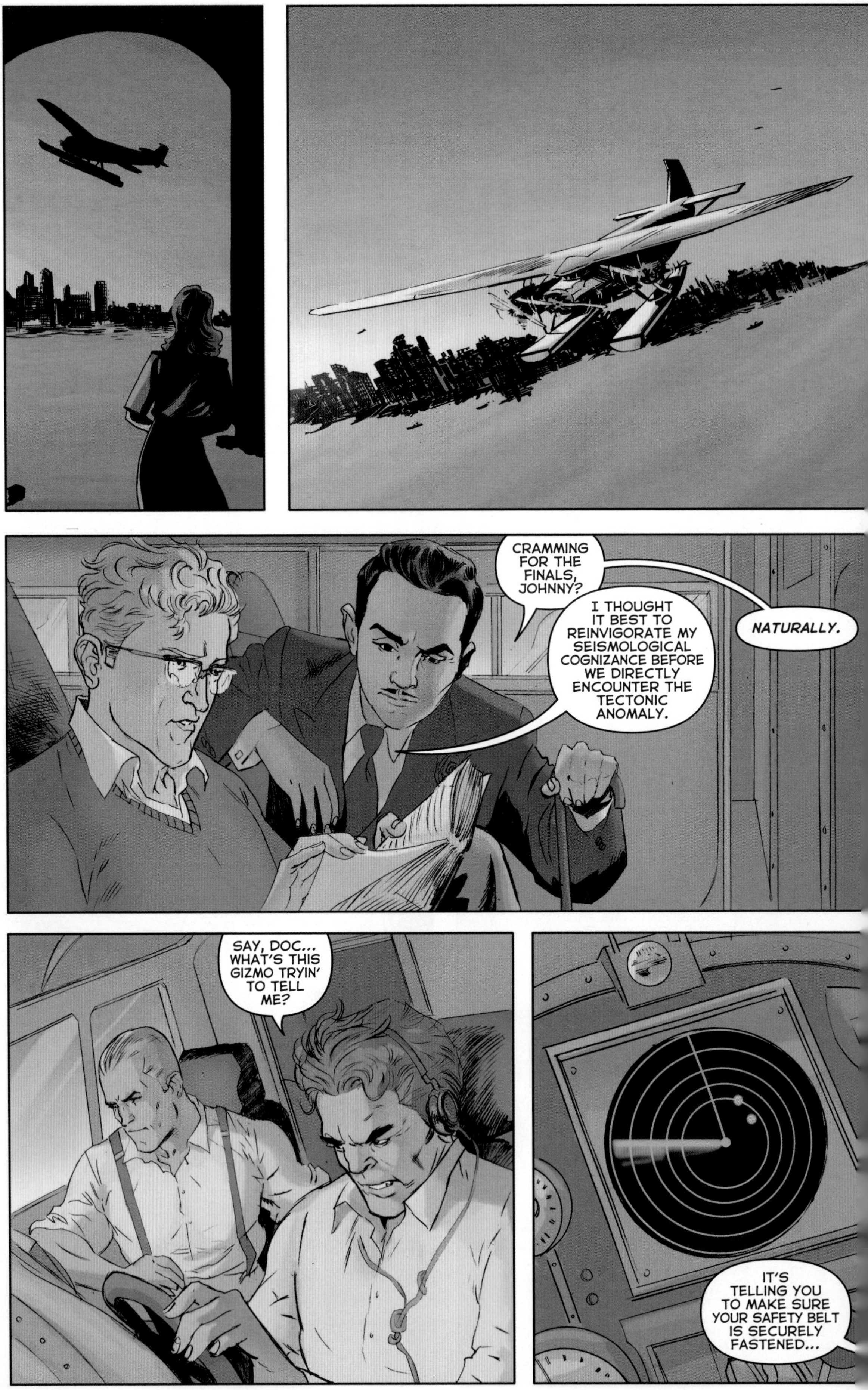
CRAMMING FOR THE FINALS, JOHNNY?
I THOUGHT IT BEST TO REINVIGORATE MY SEISMOLOGICAL COGNIZANCE BEFORE WE DIRECTLY ENCOUNTER THE TECTONIC ANOMALY.
NATURALLY.
SAY, DOC... WHAT'S THIS GIZMO TRYIN' TO TELL ME?
IT'S TELLING YOU TO MAKE SURE YOUR SAFETY BELT IS SECURELY FASTENED...

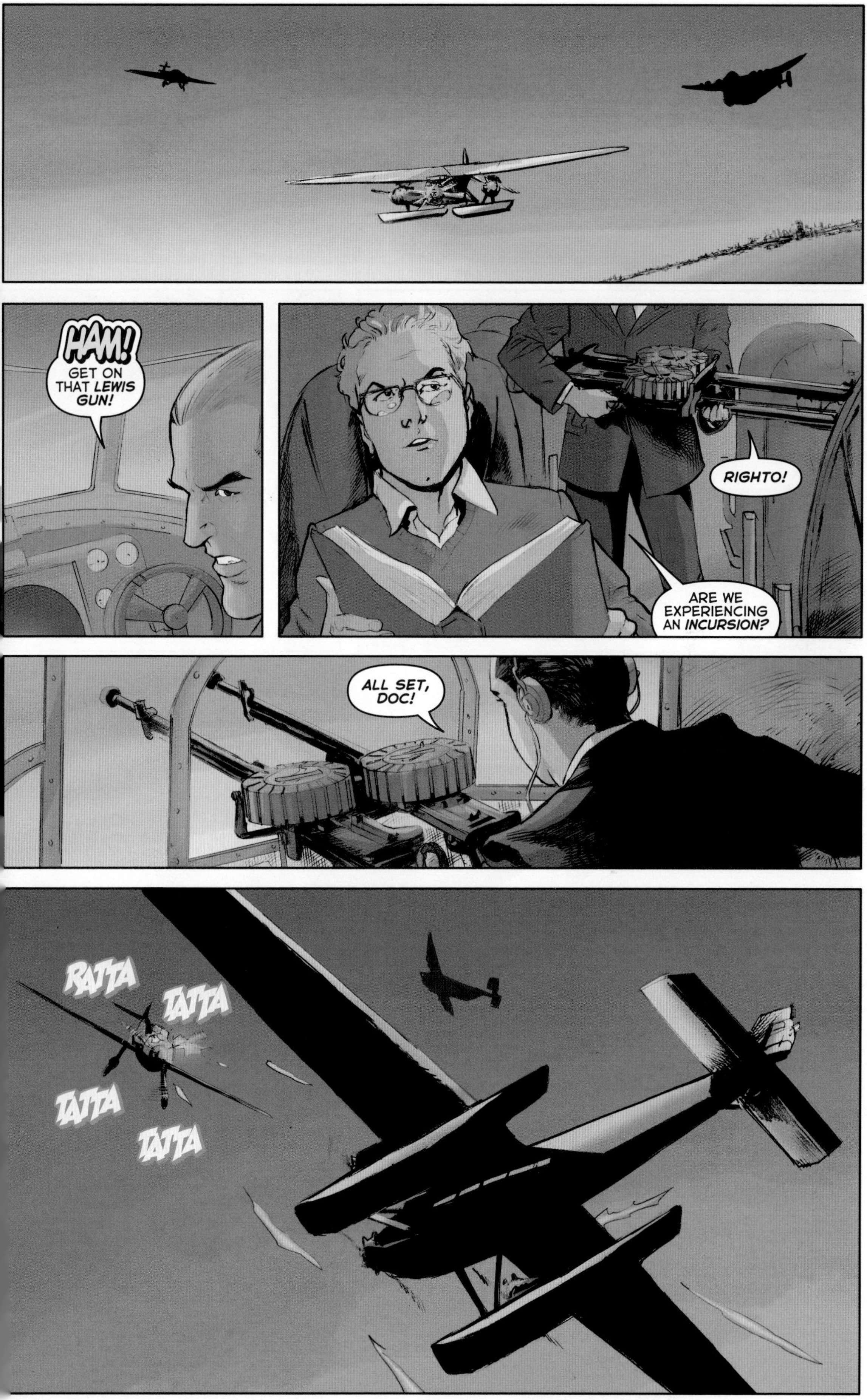
HAM!
GET ON THAT LEWIS GUN!
RIGHTO!
ARE WE EXPERIENCING AN INCURSION?
ALL SET, DOC!
RATTA
TATTA
TATTA
TATTA

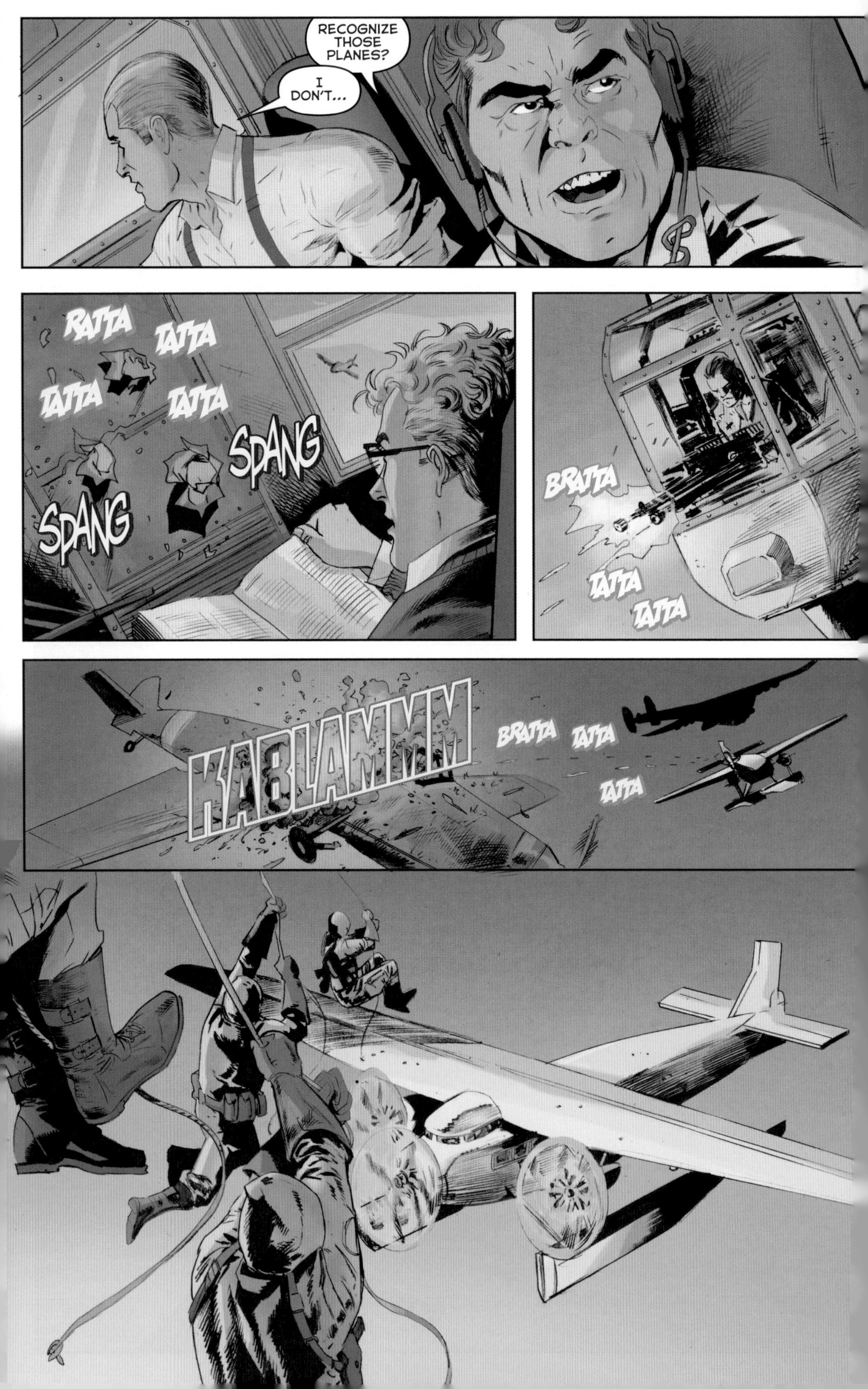
RECOGNIZE THOSE PLANES?
I DON'T...
RATTA
TATTA
TATTA
TATTA
SPANG
SPANG
BRATTA
TATTA
TATTA
KABLAMMM
BRATTA
TATTA
TATTA

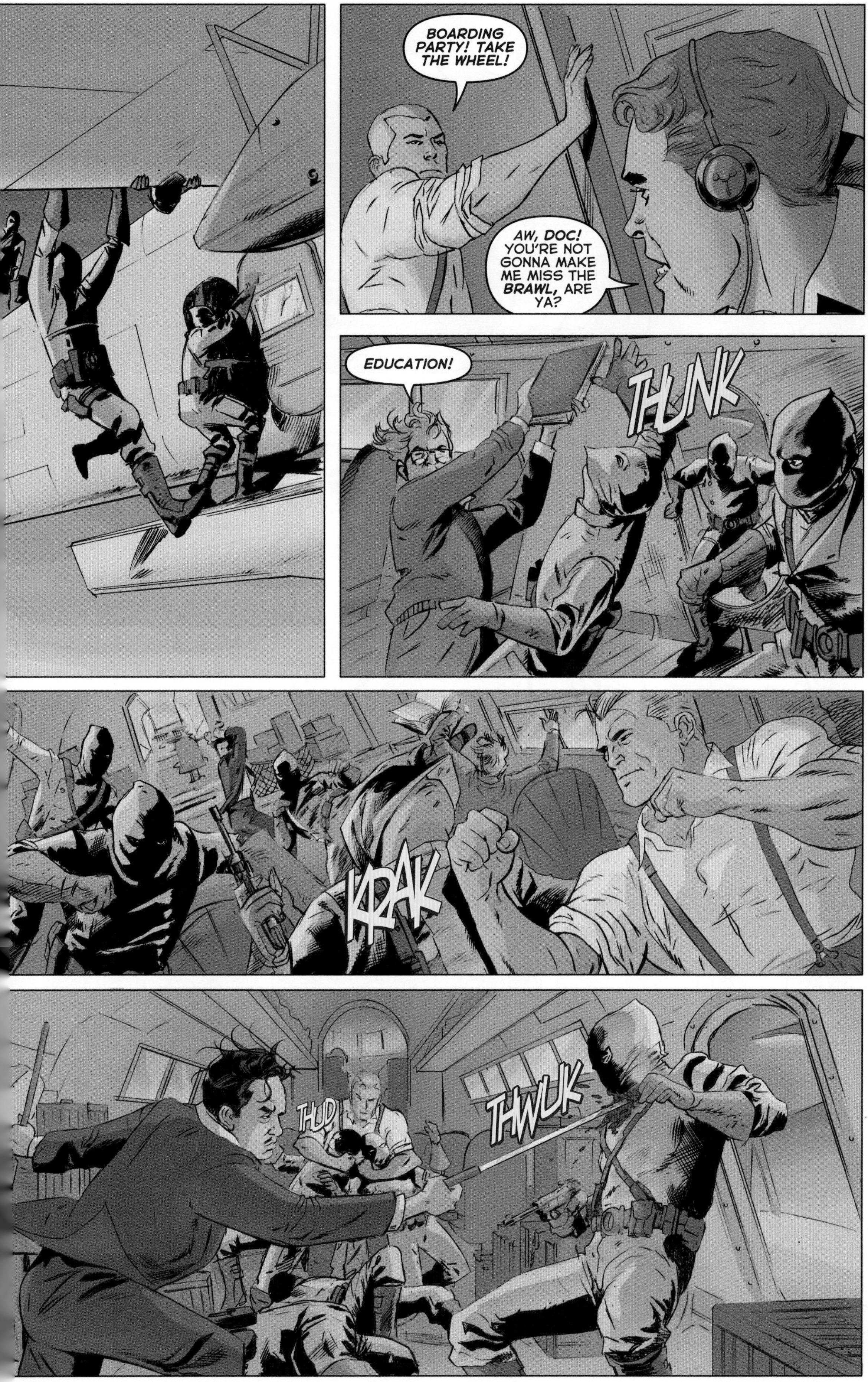
BOARDING PARTY! TAKE THE WHEEL!
AW, DOC! YOU'RE NOT GONNA MAKE ME MISS THE BRAWL, ARE YA?
EDUCATION!
THUNK
KRAK
THUD
THWUK

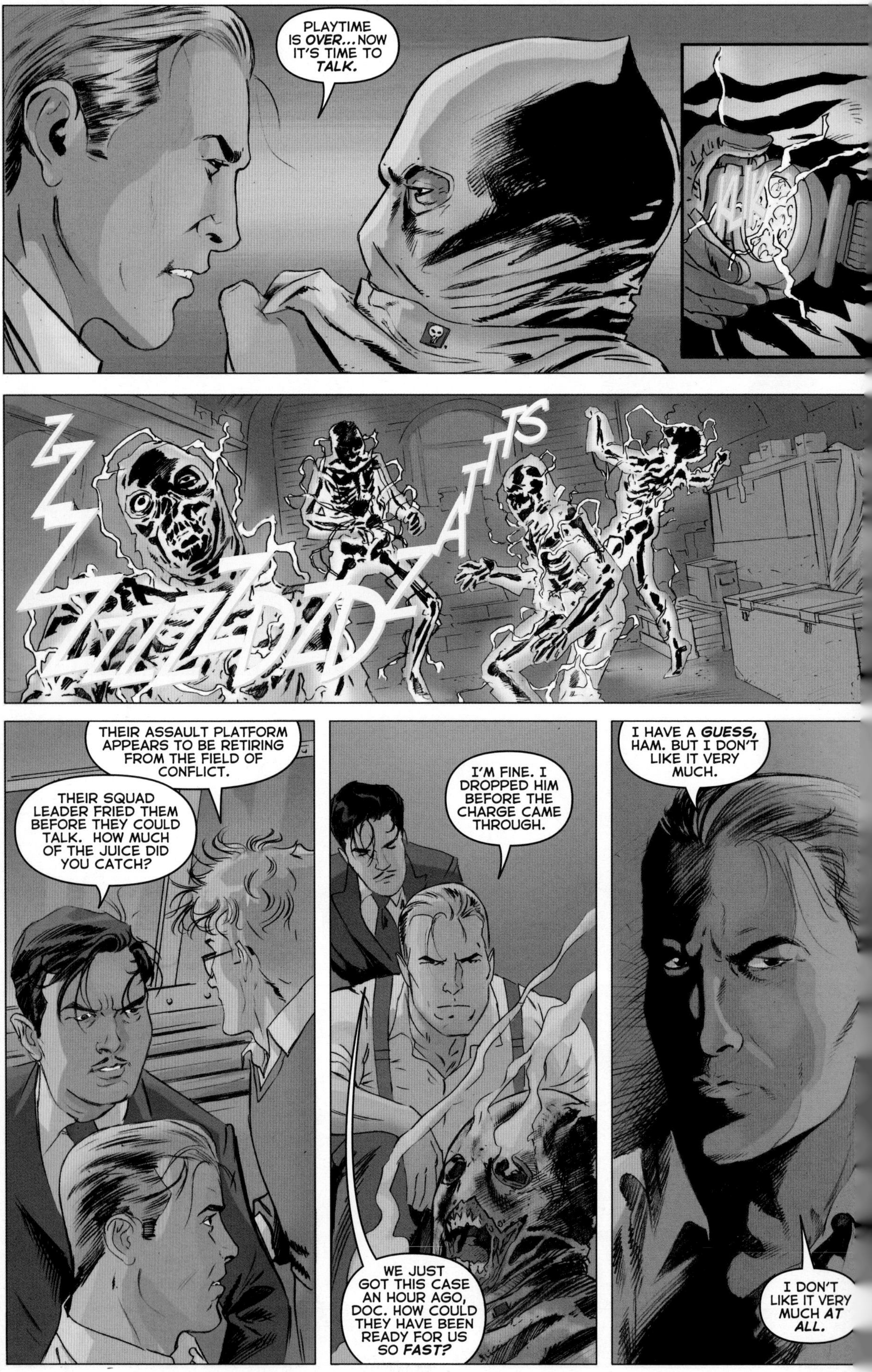
PLAYTIME IS *OVER...* NOW IT'S TIME TO *TALK.*
KLIK
THEIR ASSAULT PLATFORM APPEARS TO BE RETIRING FROM THE FIELD OF CONFLICT.
THEIR SQUAD LEADER FRIED THEM BEFORE THEY COULD TALK. HOW MUCH OF THE JUICE DID YOU CATCH?
I'M FINE. I DROPPED HIM BEFORE THE CHARGE CAME THROUGH.
WE JUST GOT THIS CASE AN HOUR AGO, DOC. HOW COULD THEY HAVE BEEN READY FOR US SO *FAST?*
I HAVE A *GUESS,* HAM. BUT I DON'T LIKE IT VERY MUCH.
I DON'T LIKE IT VERY MUCH *AT ALL.*

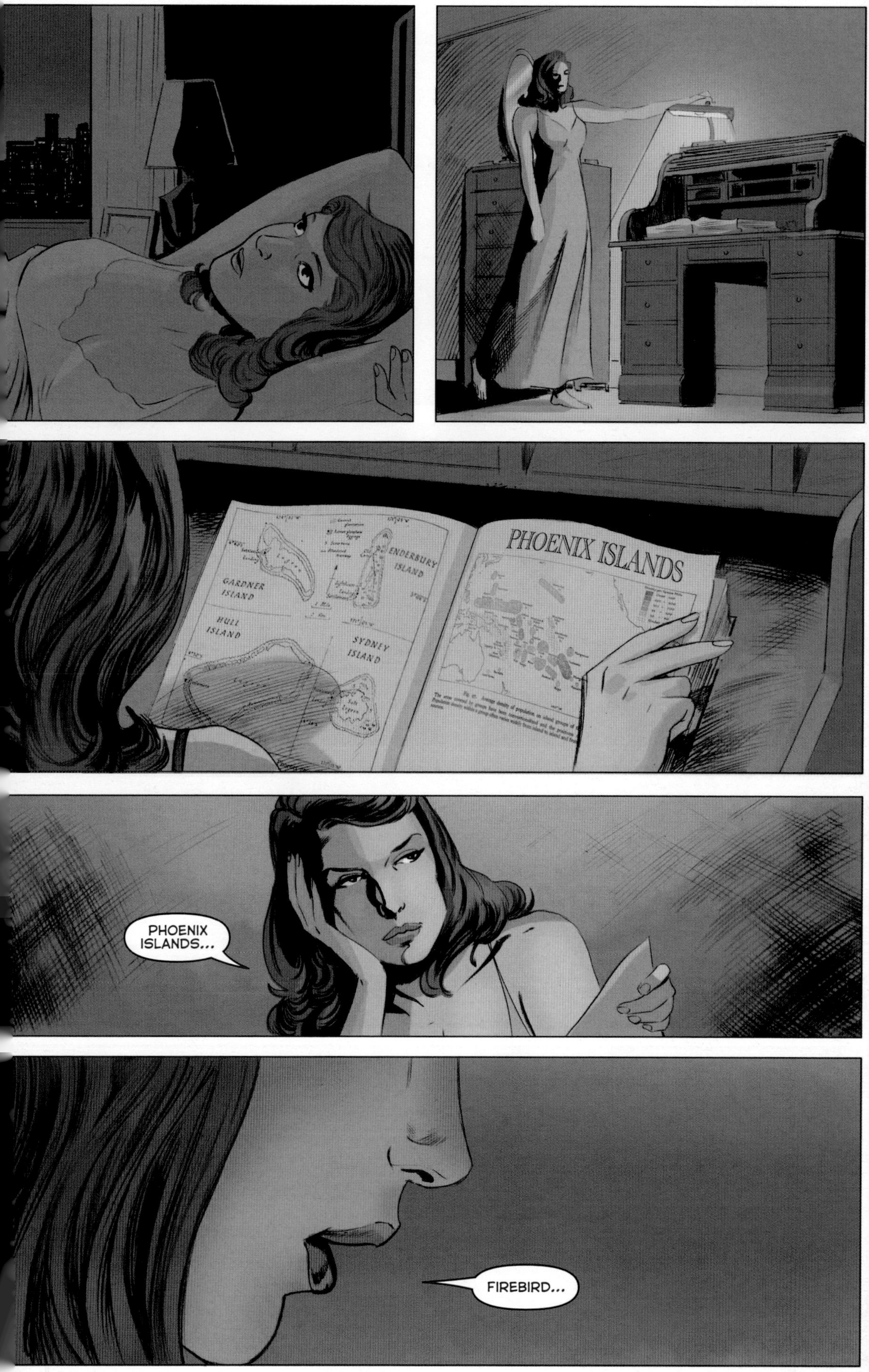
PHOENIX ISLANDS
GARDNER ISLAND
ENDERBURY ISLAND
HULL ISLAND
SYDNEY ISLAND
PHOENIX ISLANDS...
FIREBIRD...

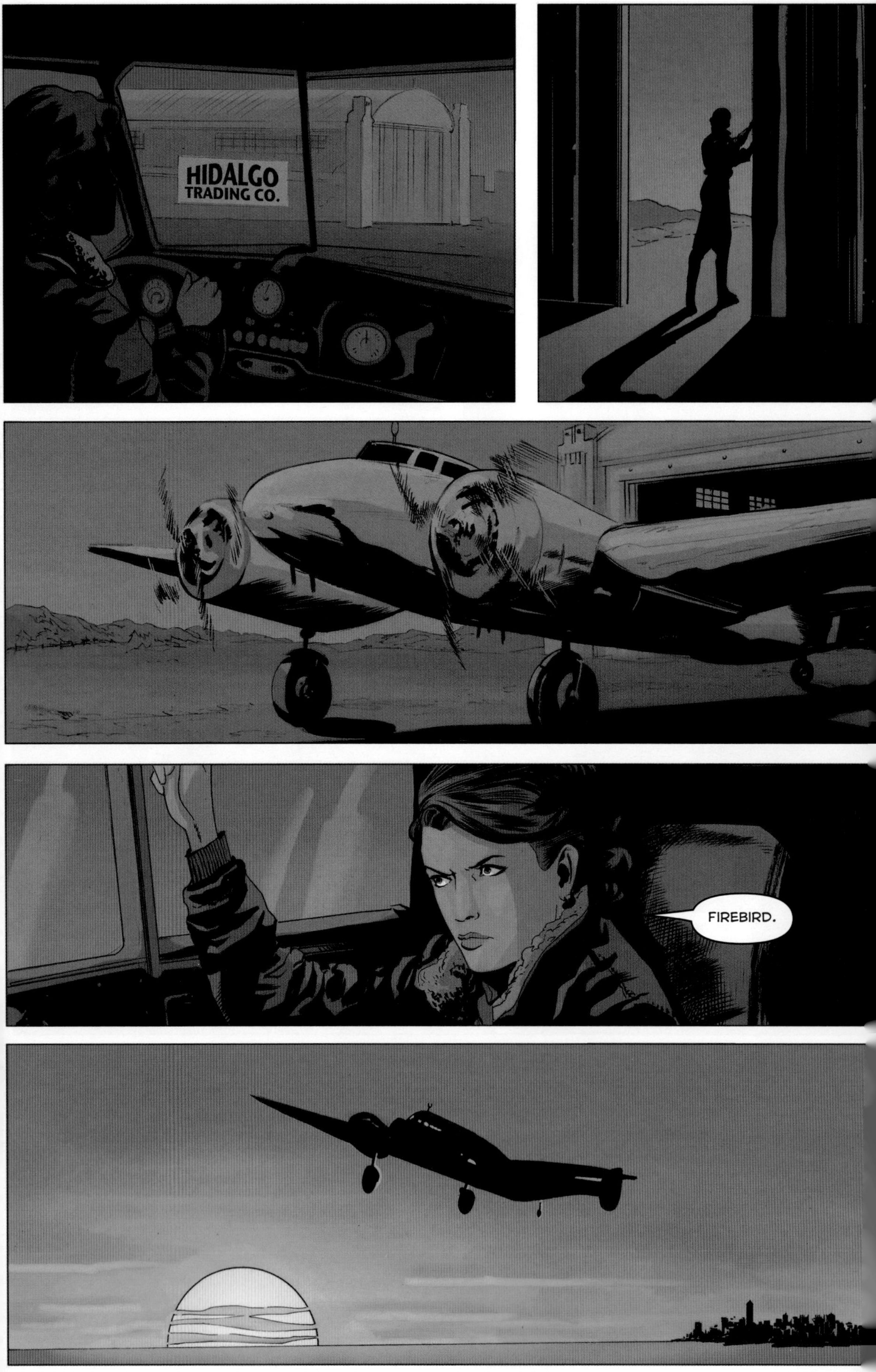
HIDALGO
TRADING CO.
FIREBIRD.

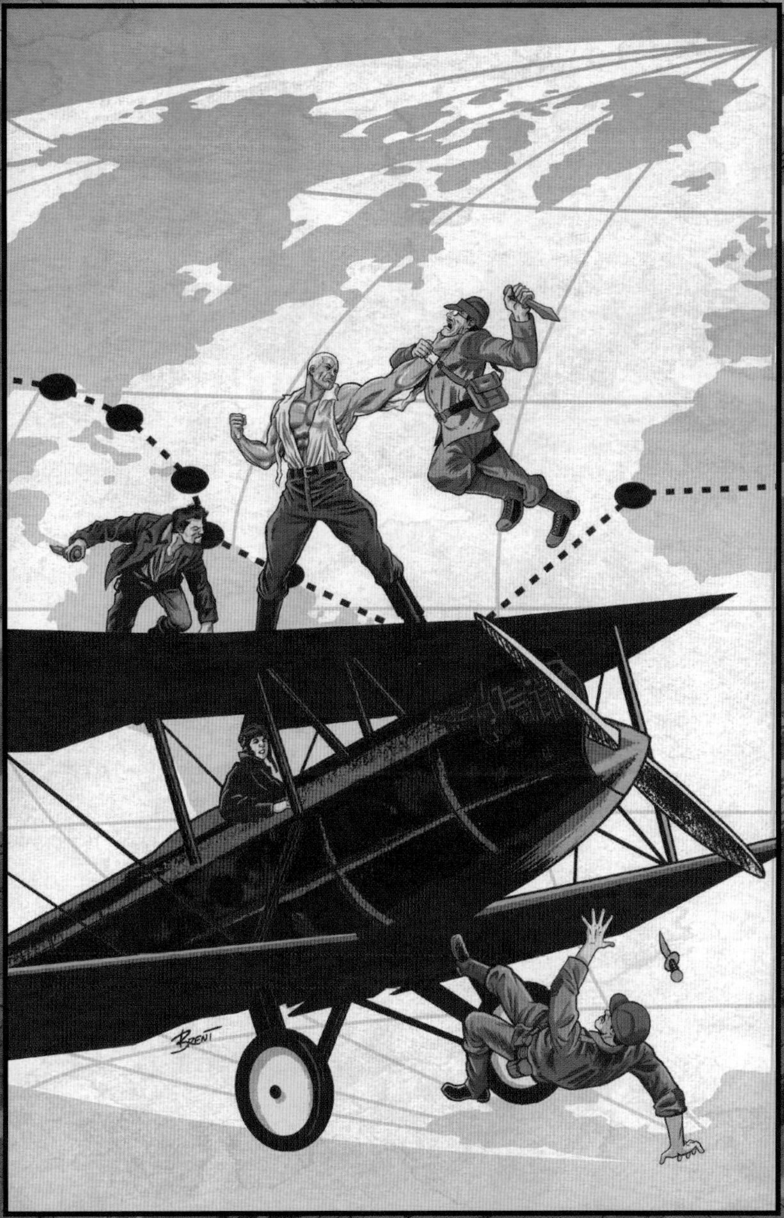
BRENT

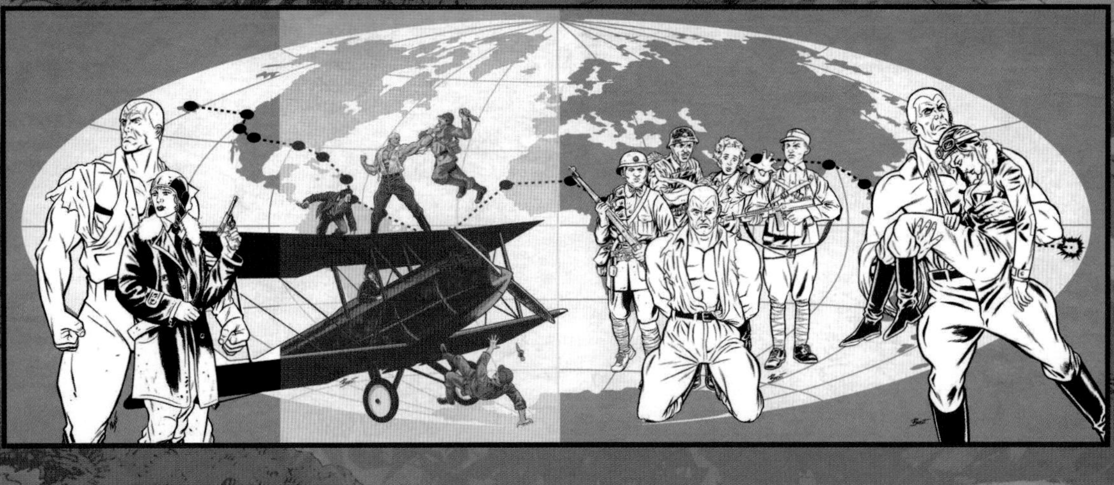

ISSUE TWO CONNECTING COVER ART BY BRENT SCHOONOVER

TWO

"ACROSS THE PACIFIC"

ISSUE TWO VARIANT COVER ART BY ANTHONY MARQUES
INKS BY J. BONE, COLORS BY CHRIS O'HALLORAN

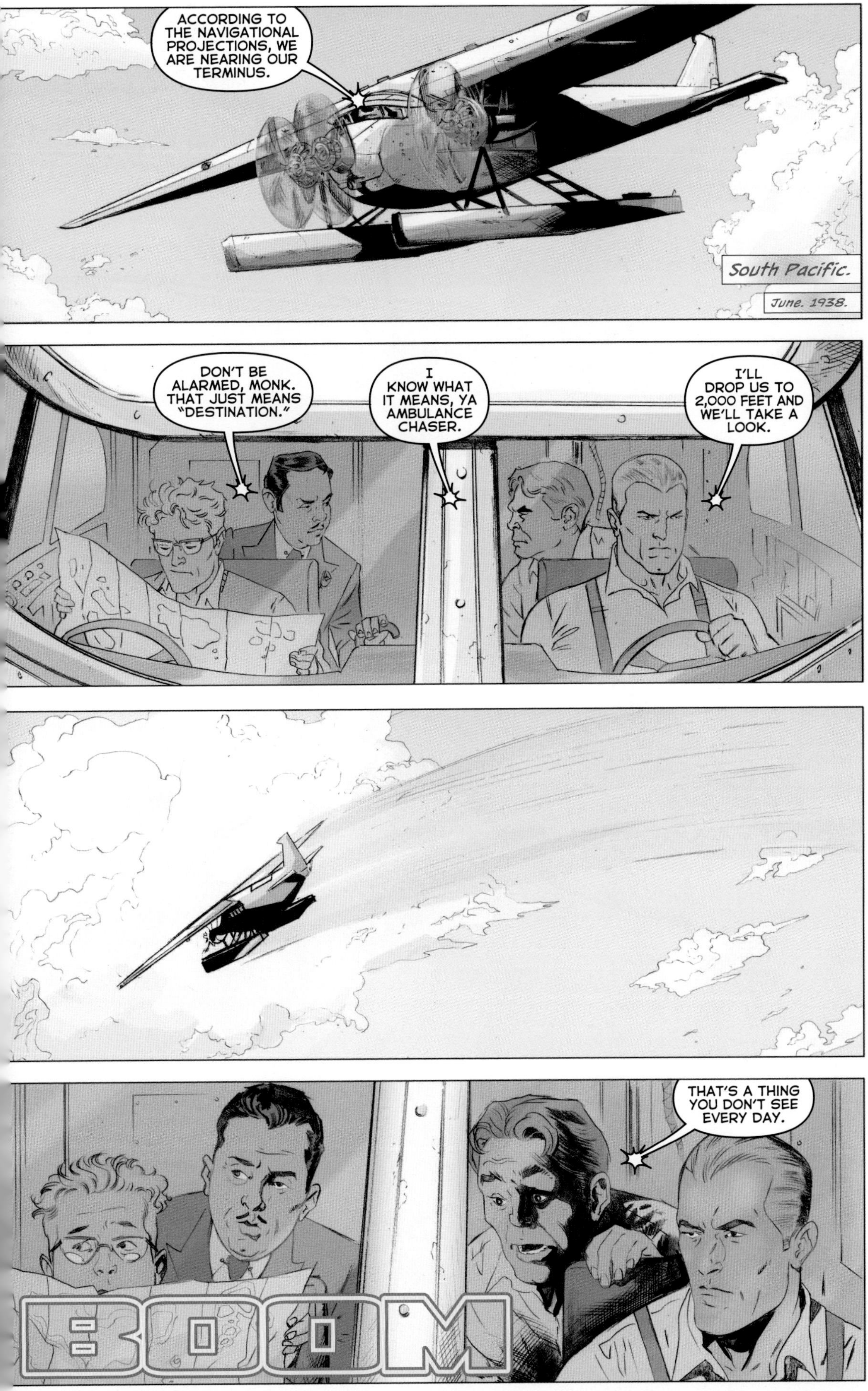
ACCORDING TO THE NAVIGATIONAL PROJECTIONS, WE ARE NEARING OUR TERMINUS.
South Pacific.
June. 1938.
DON'T BE ALARMED, MONK. THAT JUST MEANS "DESTINATION."
I KNOW WHAT IT MEANS, YA AMBULANCE CHASER.
I'LL DROP US TO 2,000 FEET AND WE'LL TAKE A LOOK.
THAT'S A THING YOU DON'T SEE EVERY DAY.
BOOM

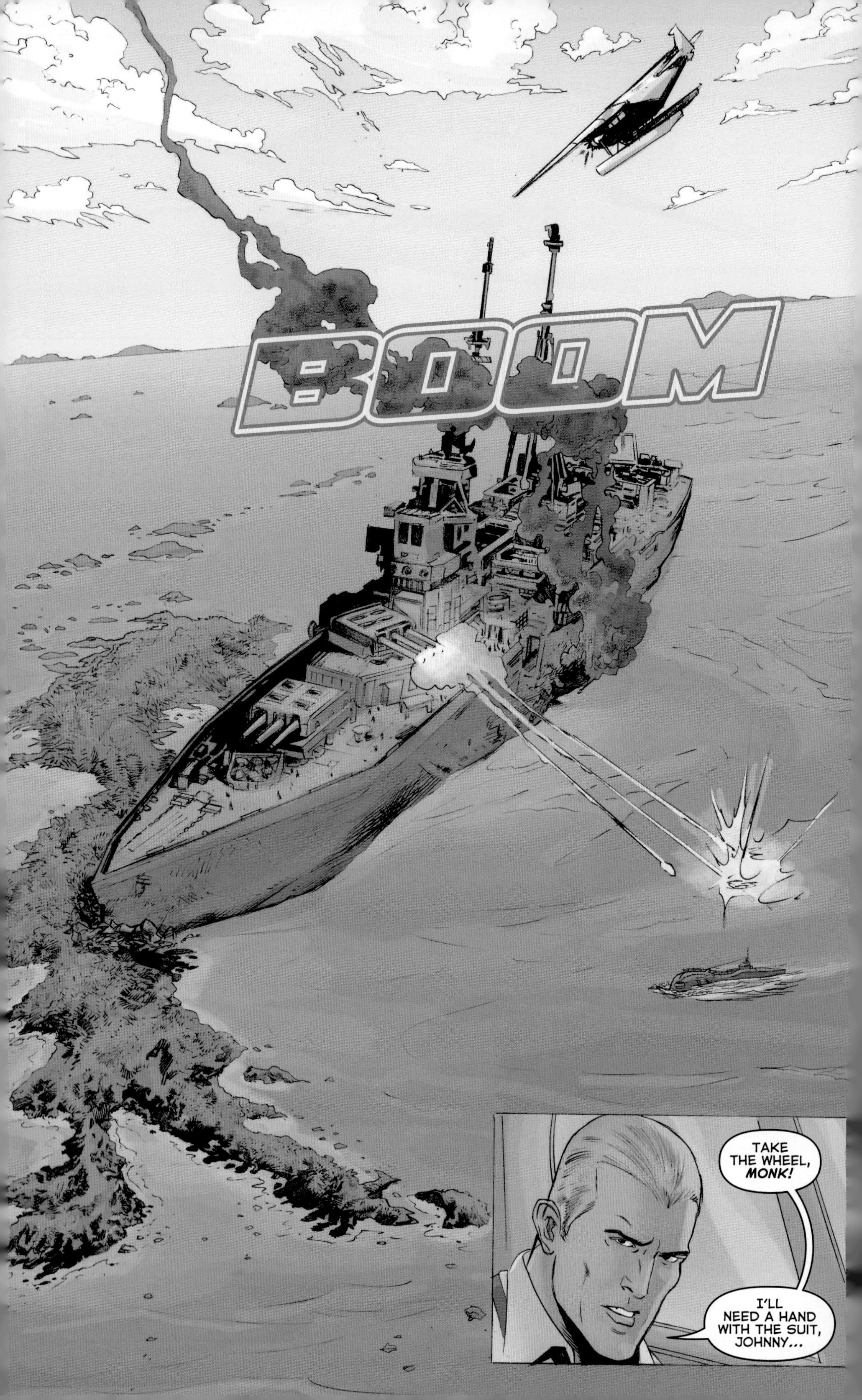
BOOM
TAKE THE WHEEL, MONK!
I'LL NEED A HAND WITH THE SUIT, JOHNNY...

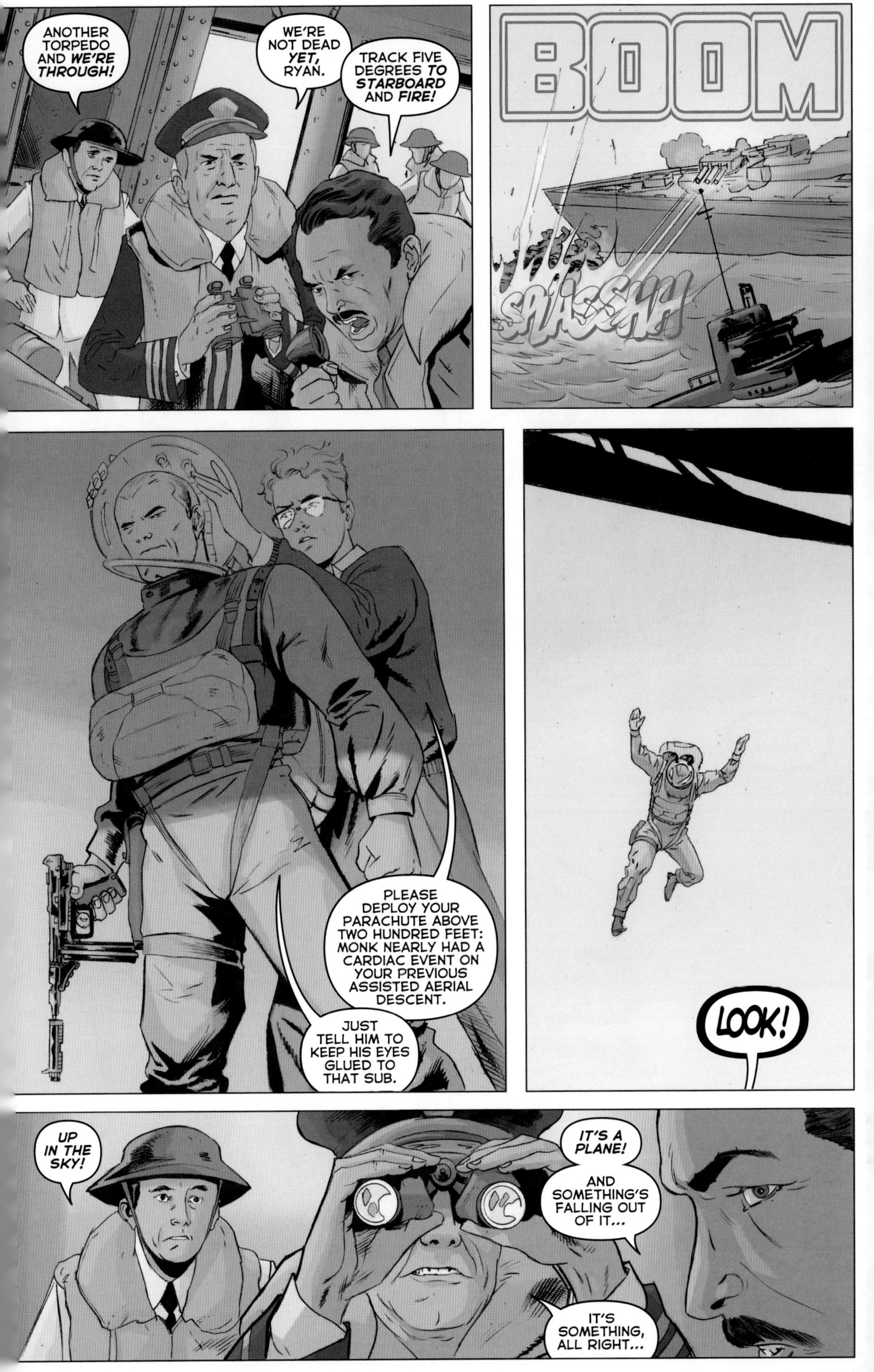
ANOTHER TORPEDO AND WE'RE THROUGH!
WE'RE NOT DEAD YET, RYAN.
TRACK FIVE DEGREES TO STARBOARD AND FIRE!
BOOM
SPLASSHH
PLEASE DEPLOY YOUR PARACHUTE ABOVE TWO HUNDRED FEET: MONK NEARLY HAD A CARDIAC EVENT ON YOUR PREVIOUS ASSISTED AERIAL DESCENT.
JUST TELL HIM TO KEEP HIS EYES GLUED TO THAT SUB.
LOOK!
UP IN THE SKY!
IT'S A PLANE!
AND SOMETHING'S FALLING OUT OF IT...
IT'S SOMETHING, ALL RIGHT...

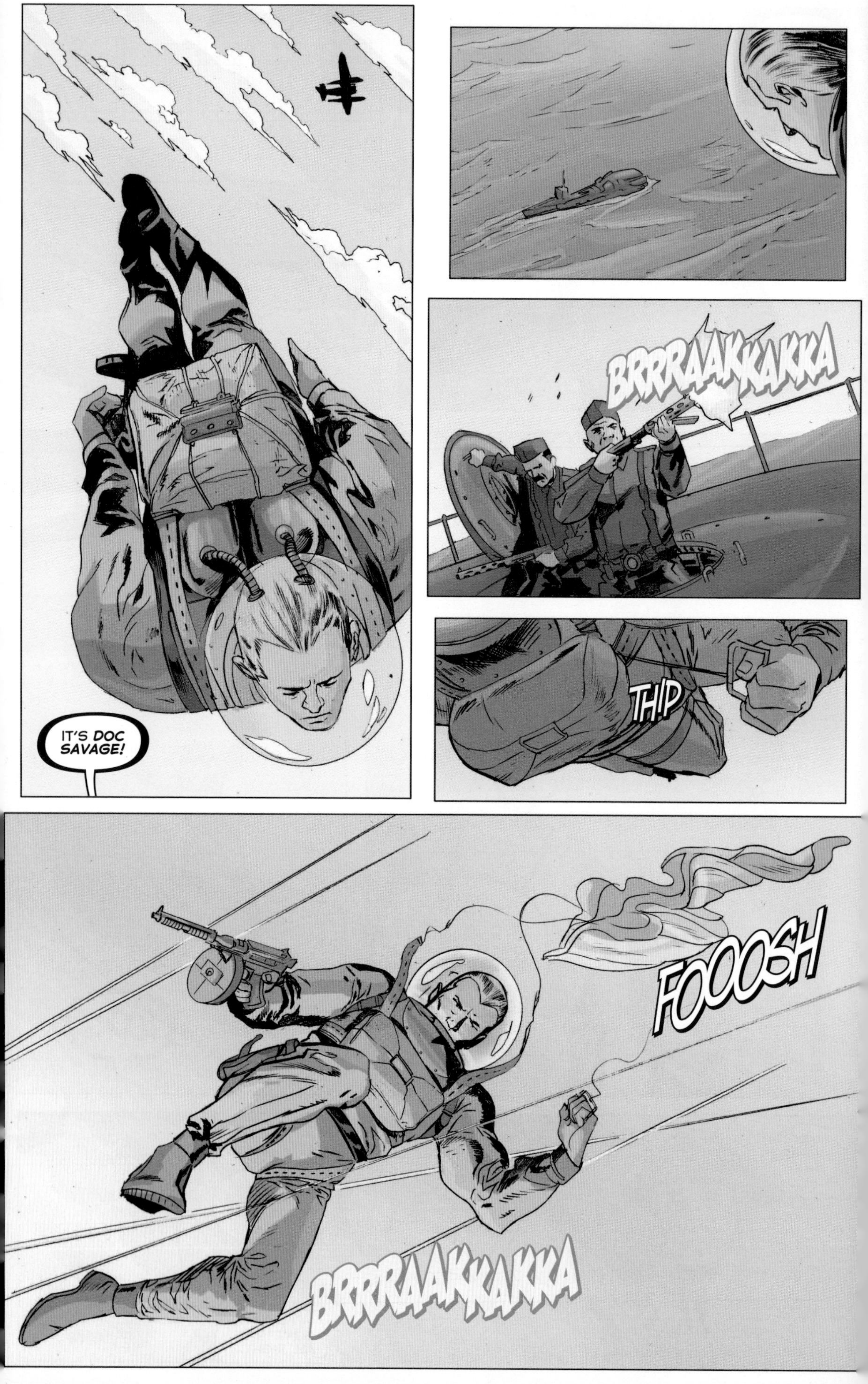
IT'S DOC SAVAGE!
BRRRAAKKAKKA
THIP
FOOOSH
BRRRAAKKAKKA

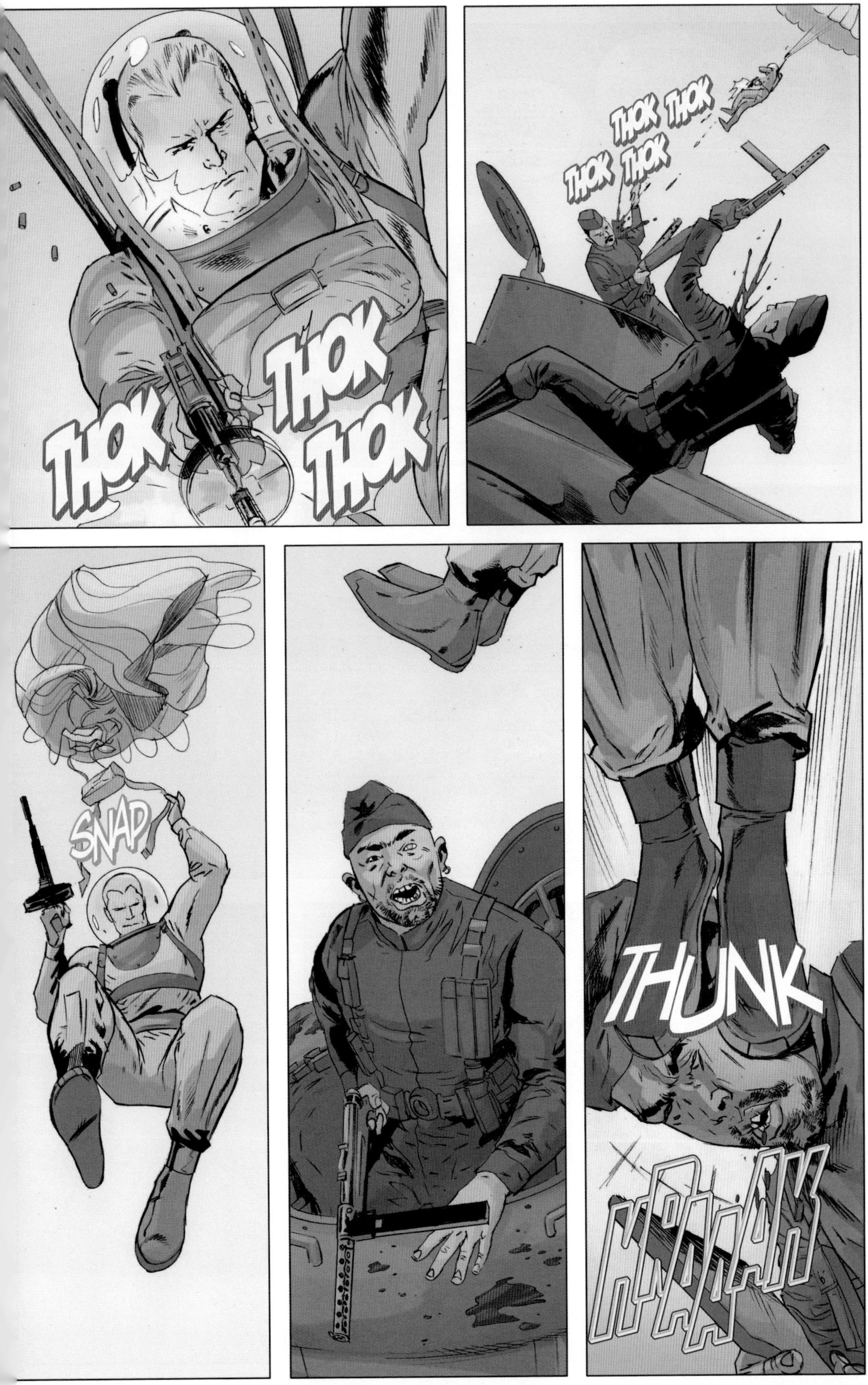
THOK THOK THOK
THOK THOK
THOK THOK
SNAP
THUNK

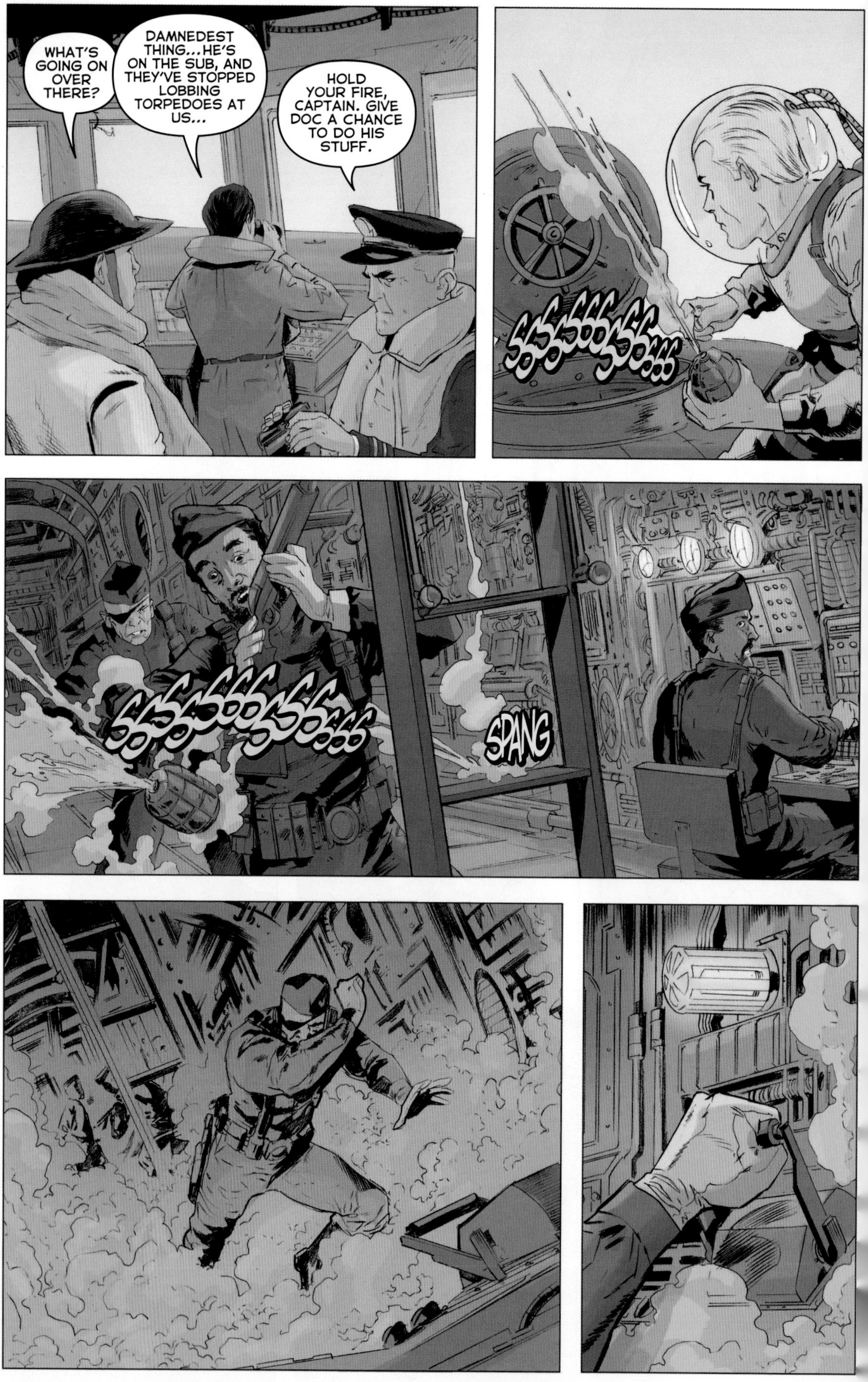
WHAT'S GOING ON OVER THERE?
DAMNEDEST THING...HE'S ON THE SUB, AND THEY'VE STOPPED LOBBING TORPEDOES AT US...
HOLD YOUR FIRE, CAPTAIN. GIVE DOC A CHANCE TO DO HIS STUFF.
SSSSSSSSSSSSS
SSSSSSSSSSSSSSSS
SPANG

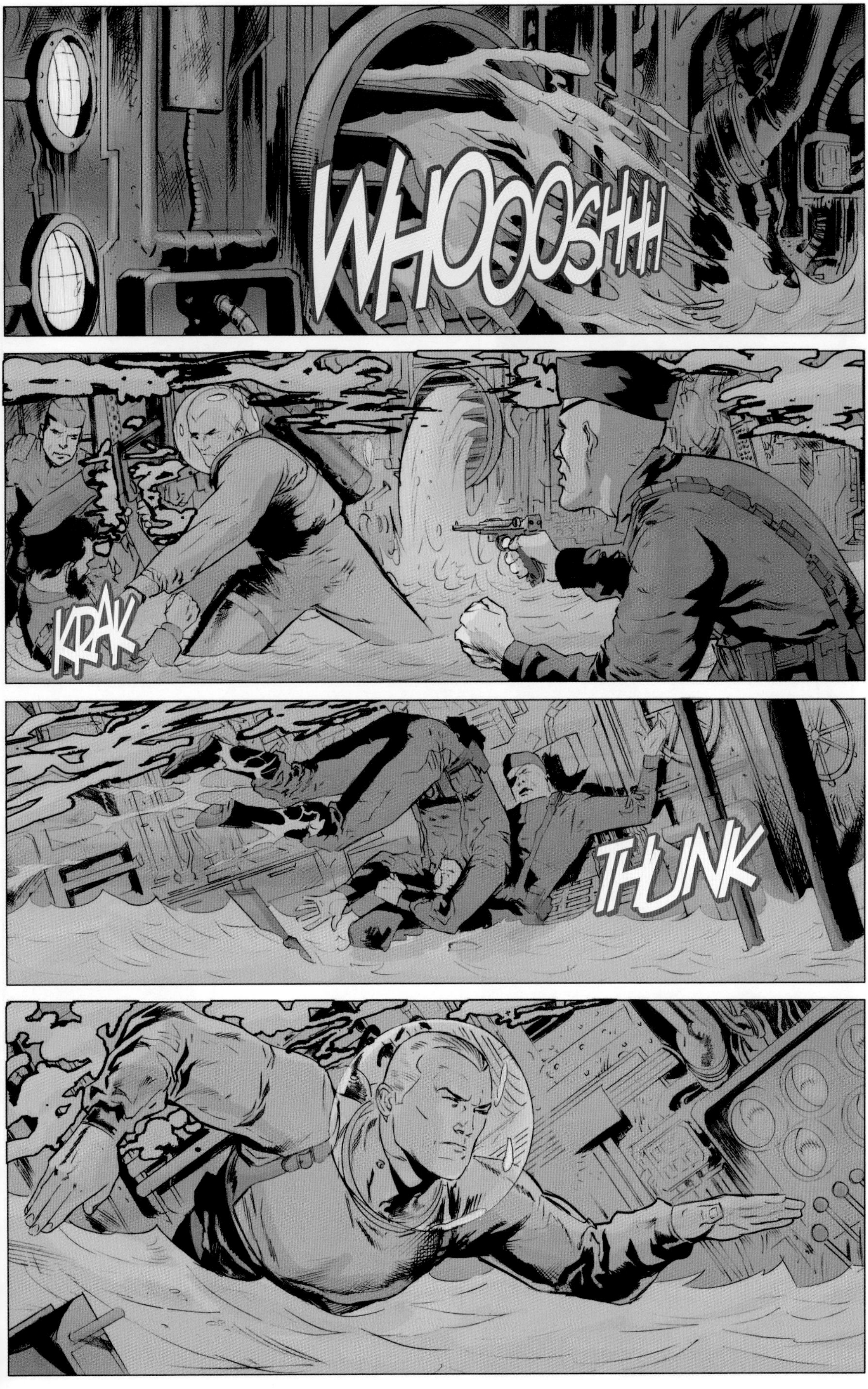
WHOOOSHHH
KRAK
THUNK

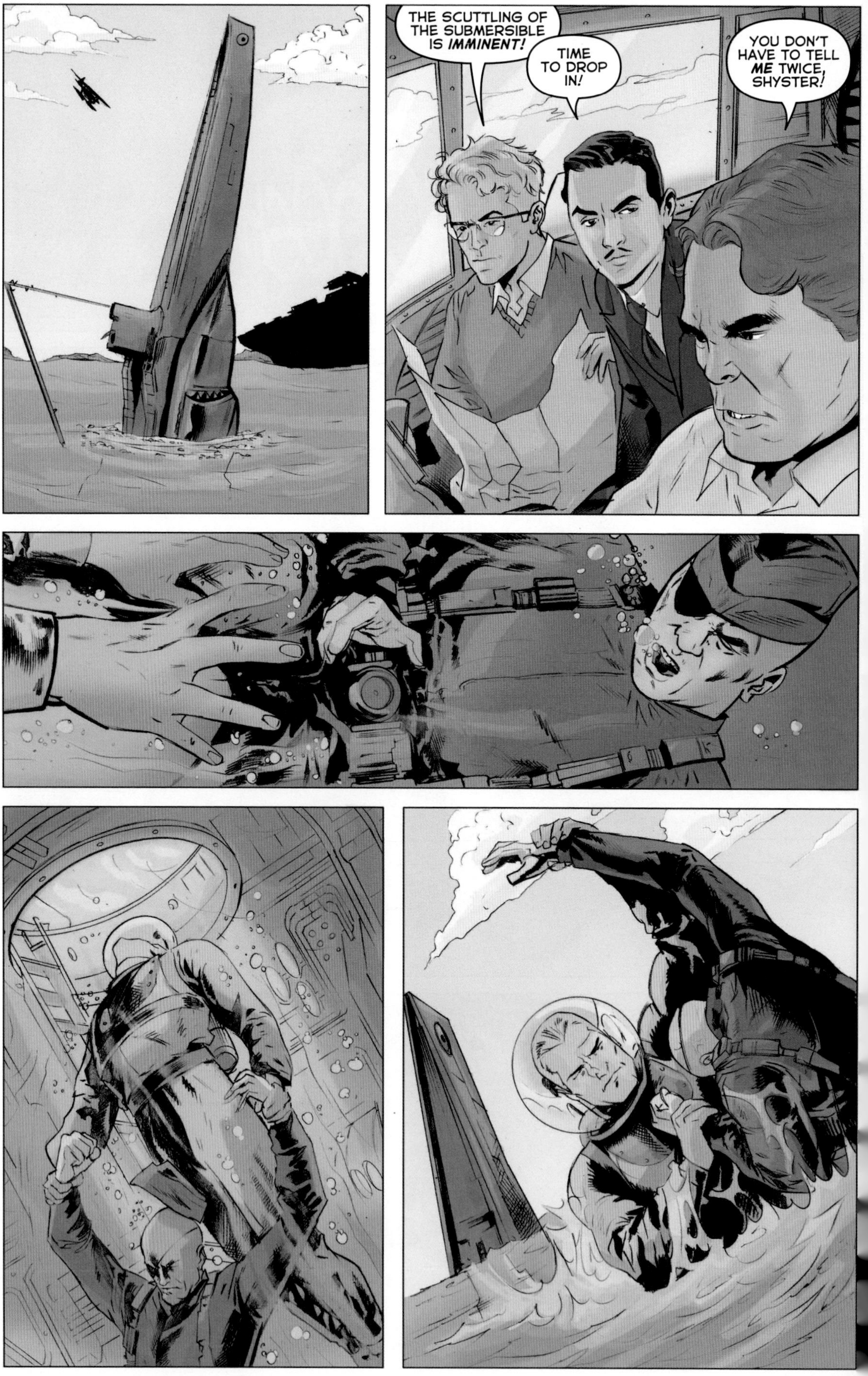
THE SCUTTLING OF THE SUBMERSIBLE IS *IMMINENT!*
TIME TO DROP IN!
YOU DON'T HAVE TO TELL *ME* TWICE, SHYSTER!

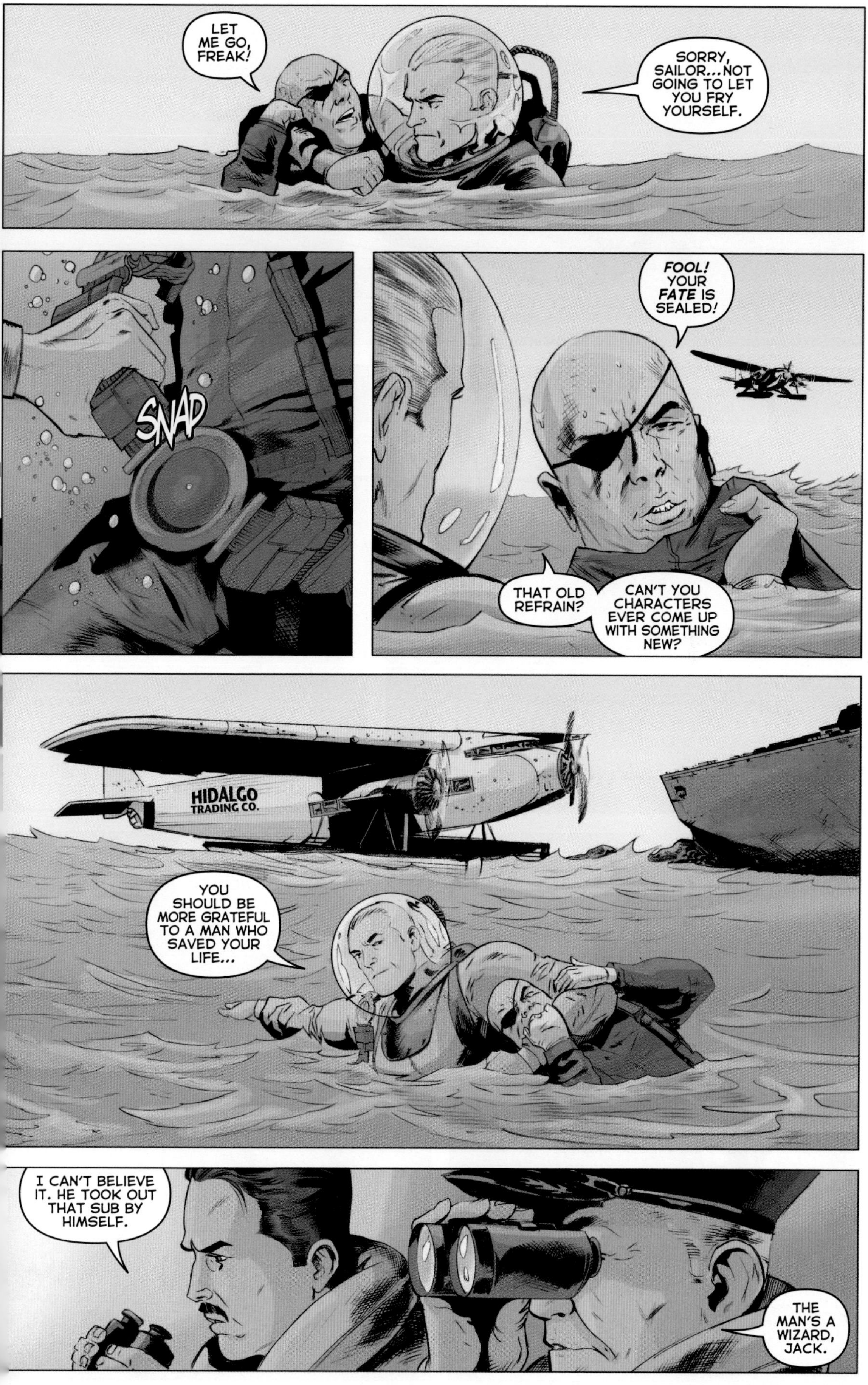
LET ME GO, FREAK!
SORRY, SAILOR...NOT GOING TO LET YOU FRY YOURSELF.
SNAP
FOOL! YOUR FATE IS SEALED!
THAT OLD REFRAIN?
CAN'T YOU CHARACTERS EVER COME UP WITH SOMETHING NEW?
HIDALGO TRADING CO.
YOU SHOULD BE MORE GRATEFUL TO A MAN WHO SAVED YOUR LIFE...
I CAN'T BELIEVE IT. HE TOOK OUT THAT SUB BY HIMSELF.
THE MAN'S A WIZARD, JACK.

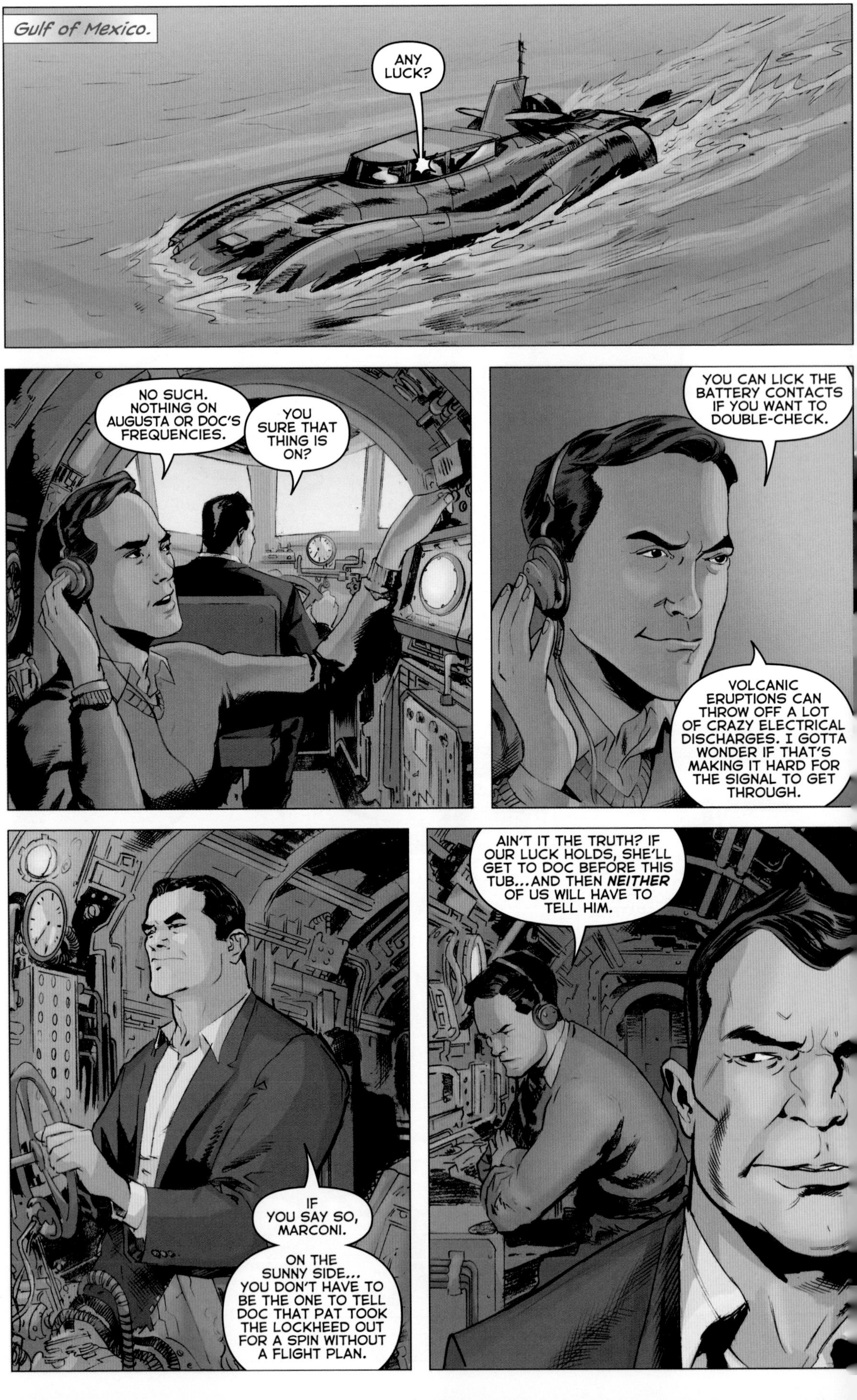
Gulf of Mexico.
ANY LUCK?
NO SUCH. NOTHING ON AUGUSTA OR DOC'S FREQUENCIES.
YOU SURE THAT THING IS ON?
YOU CAN LICK THE BATTERY CONTACTS IF YOU WANT TO DOUBLE-CHECK.
VOLCANIC ERUPTIONS CAN THROW OFF A LOT OF CRAZY ELECTRICAL DISCHARGES. I GOTTA WONDER IF THAT'S MAKING IT HARD FOR THE SIGNAL TO GET THROUGH.
IF YOU SAY SO, MARCONI.
ON THE SUNNY SIDE... YOU DON'T HAVE TO BE THE ONE TO TELL DOC THAT PAT TOOK THE LOCKHEED OUT FOR A SPIN WITHOUT A FLIGHT PLAN.
AIN'T IT THE TRUTH? IF OUR LUCK HOLDS, SHE'LL GET TO DOC BEFORE THIS TUB...AND THEN *NEITHER* OF US WILL HAVE TO TELL HIM.

WHERE'S YOUR BASE, CAPTAIN?

I KNOW YOU'RE PART OF SOMETHING *BIGGER*. SOMETHING YOU WERE WILLING TO *DIE* FOR.

WE'D ALL DIE AT THE MASTER'S WHIM.

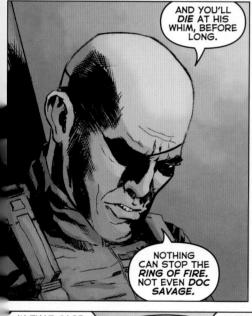

AND YOU'LL *DIE* AT HIS WHIM, BEFORE LONG.

NOTHING CAN STOP THE *RING OF FIRE*. NOT EVEN *DOC SAVAGE*.

YOU KNOW ME. YOU WERE EXPECTING ME.

OF COURSE.

THE *MASTER* WAS COUNTING ON IT.

IN THAT CASE, THE *MASTER* WON'T MIND IF YOU TELL ME WHERE TO FIND HIM. RIGHT?

WHERE IS YOUR *BASE*, CAPTAIN?

GO TO *HELL*, SAVAGE, AND MAKE A SHARP LEFT. THAT'S ALL THE DIRECTIONS YOU'LL GET FROM ME.

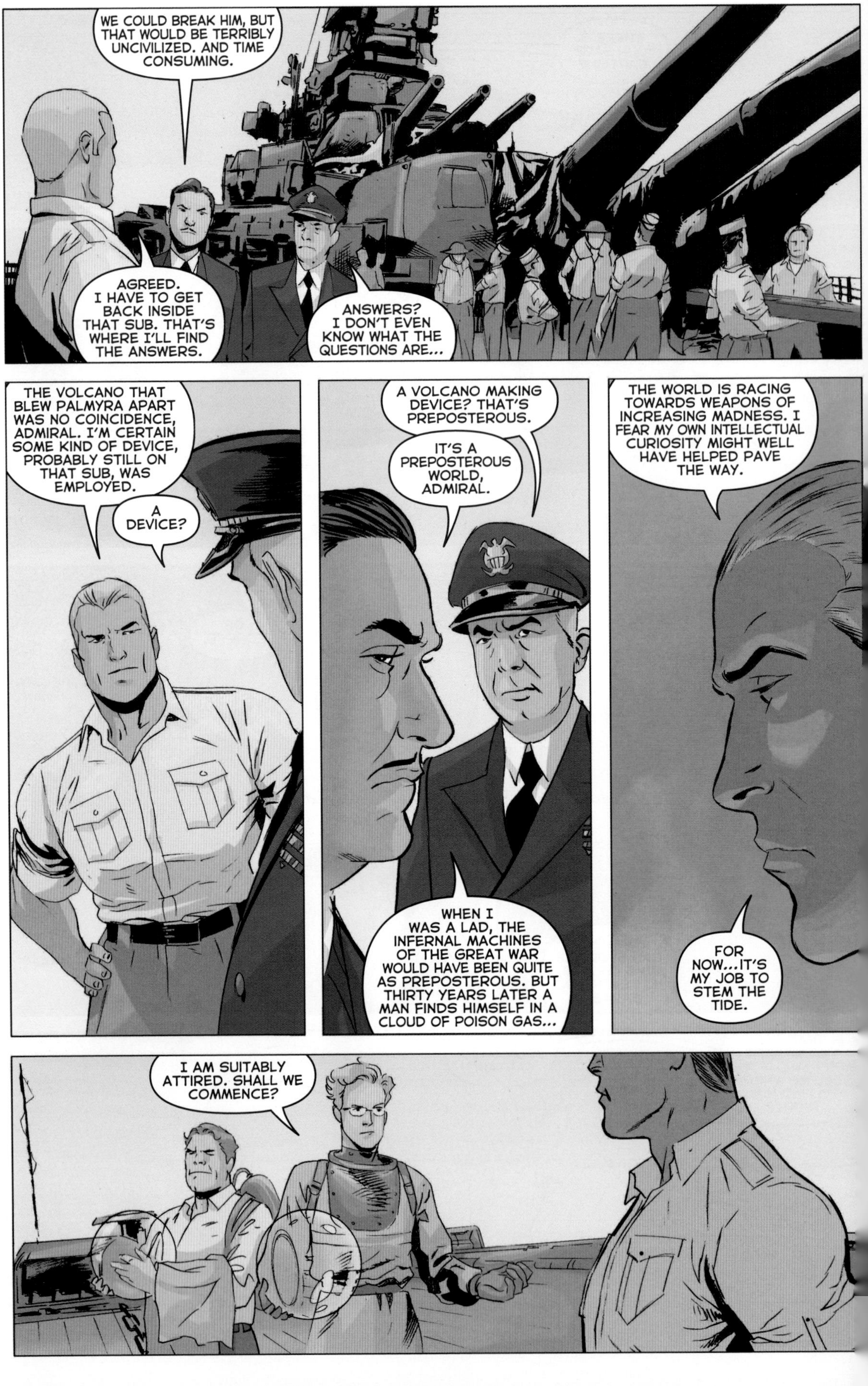
WE COULD BREAK HIM, BUT THAT WOULD BE TERRIBLY UNCIVILIZED. AND TIME CONSUMING.
AGREED. I HAVE TO GET BACK INSIDE THAT SUB. THAT'S WHERE I'LL FIND THE ANSWERS.
ANSWERS? I DON'T EVEN KNOW WHAT THE QUESTIONS ARE...
THE VOLCANO THAT BLEW PALMYRA APART WAS NO COINCIDENCE, ADMIRAL. I'M CERTAIN SOME KIND OF DEVICE, PROBABLY STILL ON THAT SUB, WAS EMPLOYED.
A DEVICE?
A VOLCANO MAKING DEVICE? THAT'S PREPOSTEROUS.
IT'S A PREPOSTEROUS WORLD, ADMIRAL.
WHEN I WAS A LAD, THE INFERNAL MACHINES OF THE GREAT WAR WOULD HAVE BEEN QUITE AS PREPOSTEROUS. BUT THIRTY YEARS LATER A MAN FINDS HIMSELF IN A CLOUD OF POISON GAS...
THE WORLD IS RACING TOWARDS WEAPONS OF INCREASING MADNESS. I FEAR MY OWN INTELLECTUAL CURIOSITY MIGHT WELL HAVE HELPED PAVE THE WAY.
FOR NOW...IT'S MY JOB TO STEM THE TIDE.
I AM SUITABLY ATTIRED. SHALL WE COMMENCE?

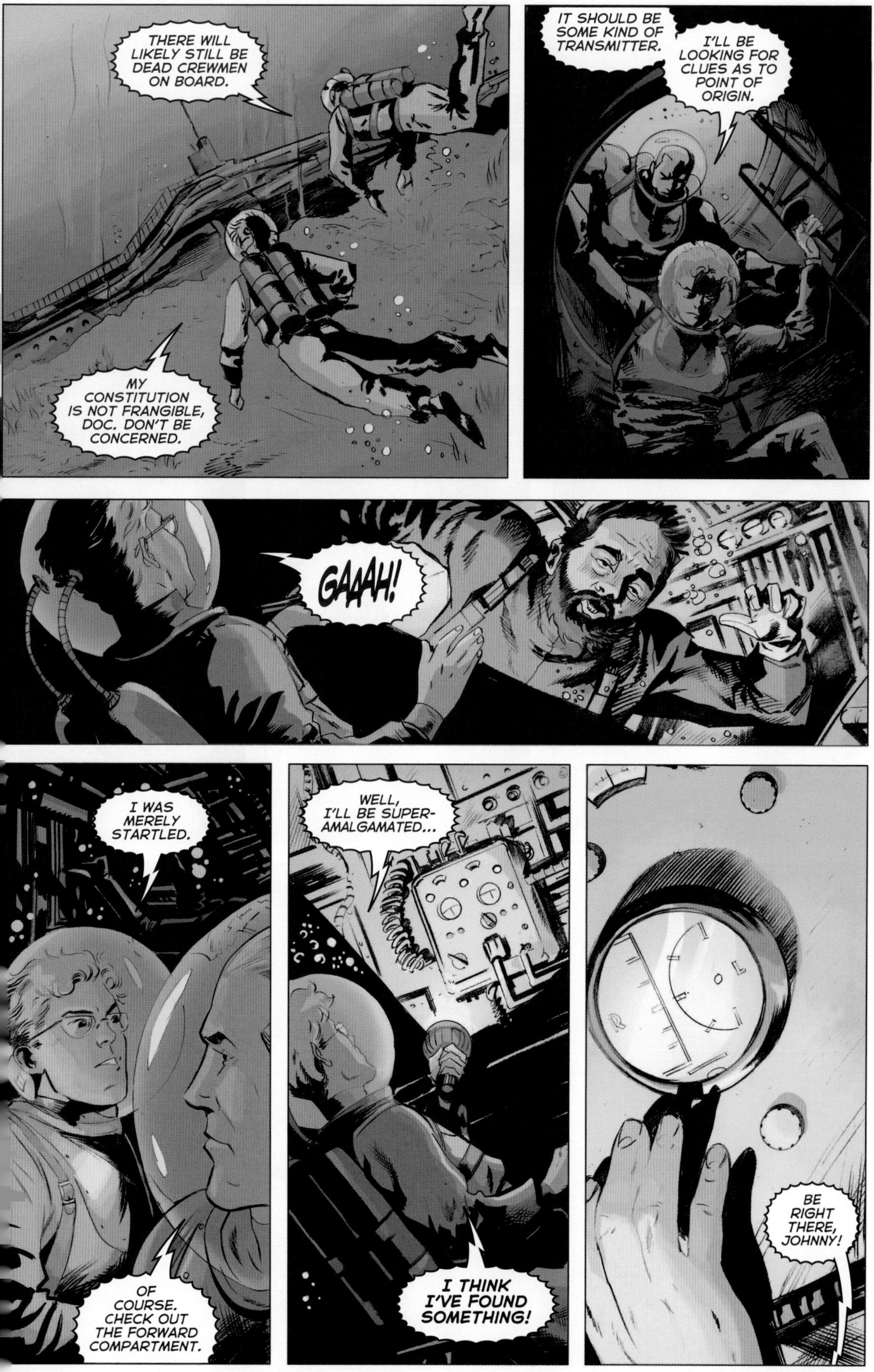
THERE WILL LIKELY STILL BE DEAD CREWMEN ON BOARD.
MY CONSTITUTION IS NOT FRANGIBLE, DOC. DON'T BE CONCERNED.
IT SHOULD BE SOME KIND OF TRANSMITTER.
I'LL BE LOOKING FOR CLUES AS TO POINT OF ORIGIN.
GAAAH!
I WAS MERELY STARTLED.
OF COURSE. CHECK OUT THE FORWARD COMPARTMENT.
WELL, I'LL BE SUPER-AMALGAMATED...
I THINK I'VE FOUND SOMETHING!
BE RIGHT THERE, JOHNNY!

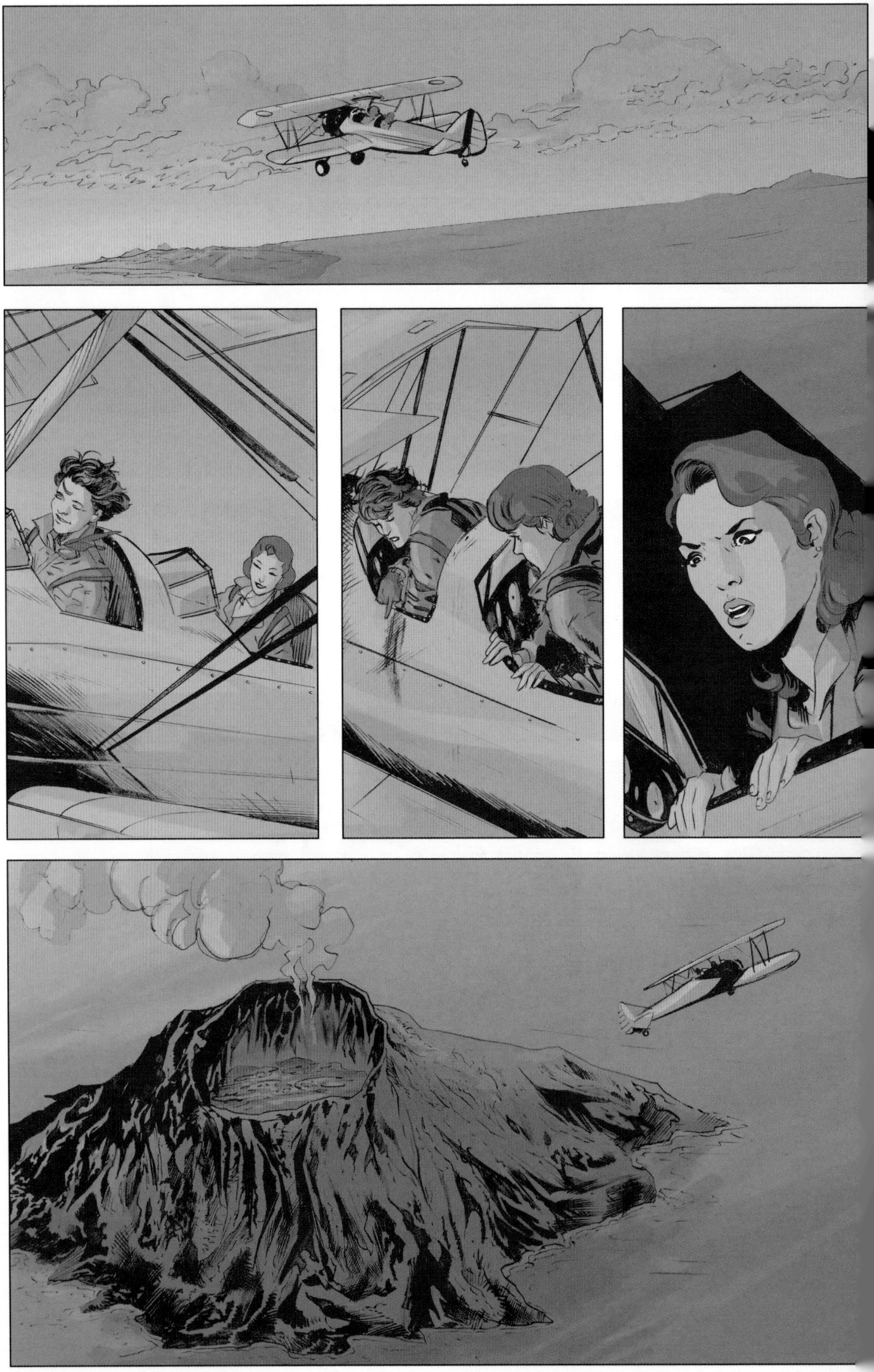

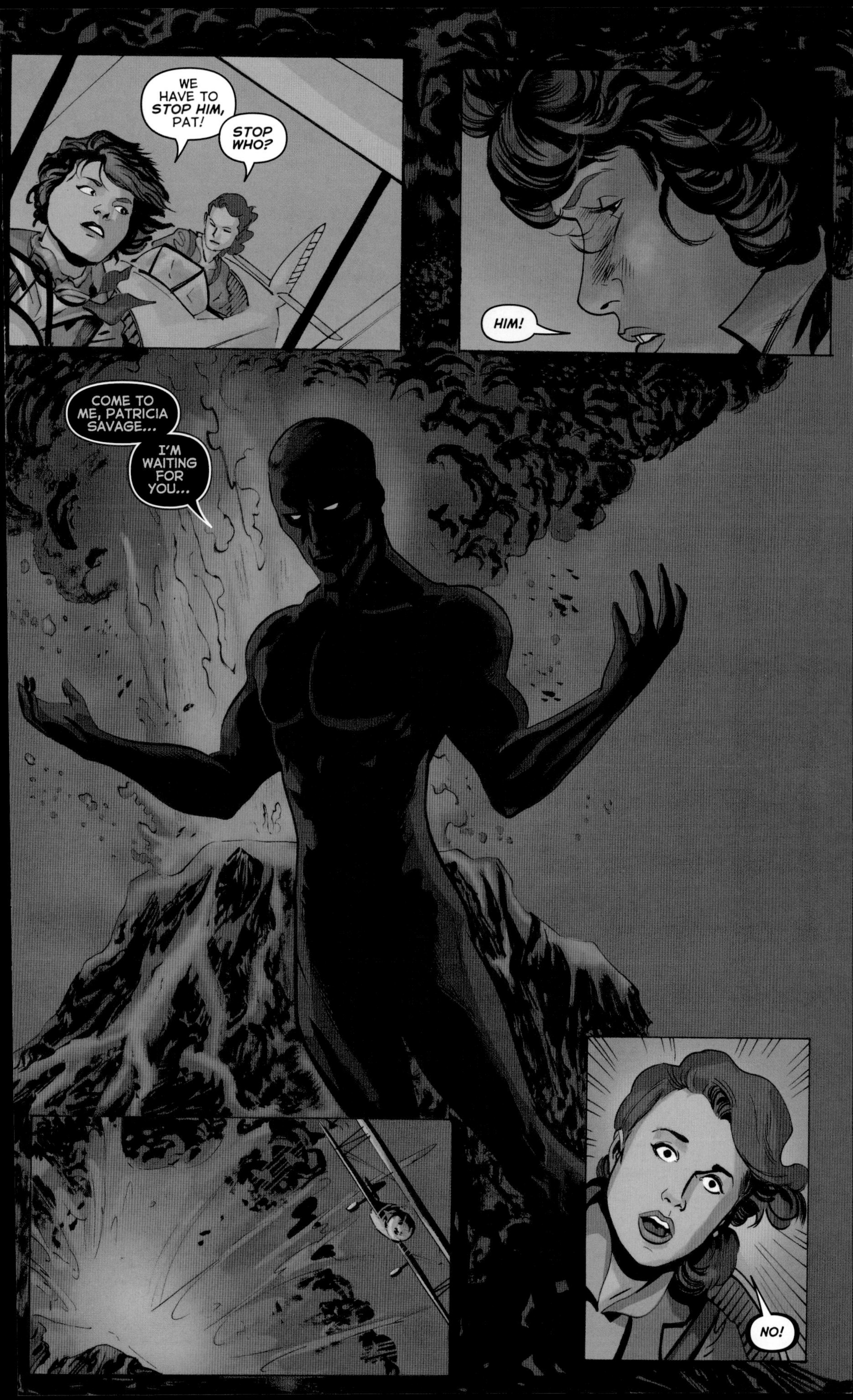
WE HAVE TO STOP HIM, PAT!
STOP WHO?
HIM!
COME TO ME, PATRICIA SAVAGE...
I'M WAITING FOR YOU...
NO!

OHHH!

I SHOULD HAVE PACKED MORE *COFFEE.*

BUT HOORAY FOR THE *AUTO-PILOT,* I GUESS.

PHOENIX ISLAND, DEAD AHEAD.

THE MAPS SHOW ROOM TO PUT THIS CRATE DOWN...

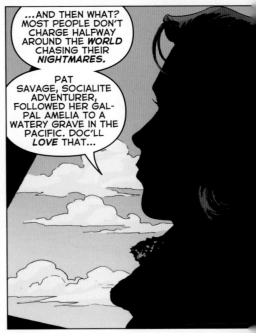

...AND THEN WHAT? MOST PEOPLE DON'T CHARGE HALFWAY AROUND THE *WORLD* CHASING THEIR *NIGHTMARES.*

PAT SAVAGE, SOCIALITE ADVENTURER, FOLLOWED HER GAL-PAL AMELIA TO A WATERY GRAVE IN THE PACIFIC. DOC'LL *LOVE* THAT...

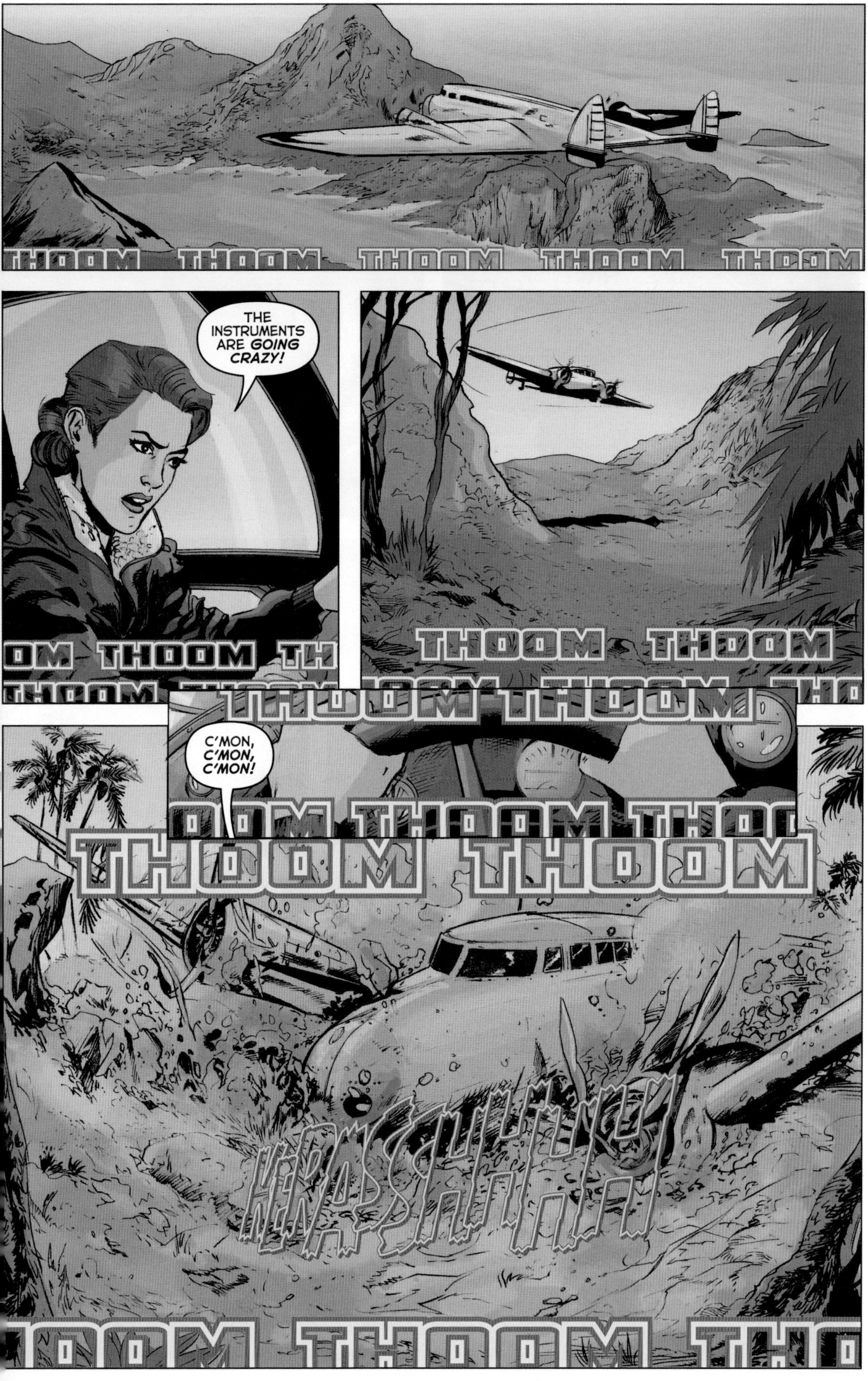
THOOM THOOM THOOM THOOM THOOM
THE INSTRUMENTS ARE GOING CRAZY!
OM THOOM TH
THOOM THOOM
THOOM THOOM
C'MON, C'MON, C'MON!
THOOM THOOM
KRASHHHHH
THOOM THO

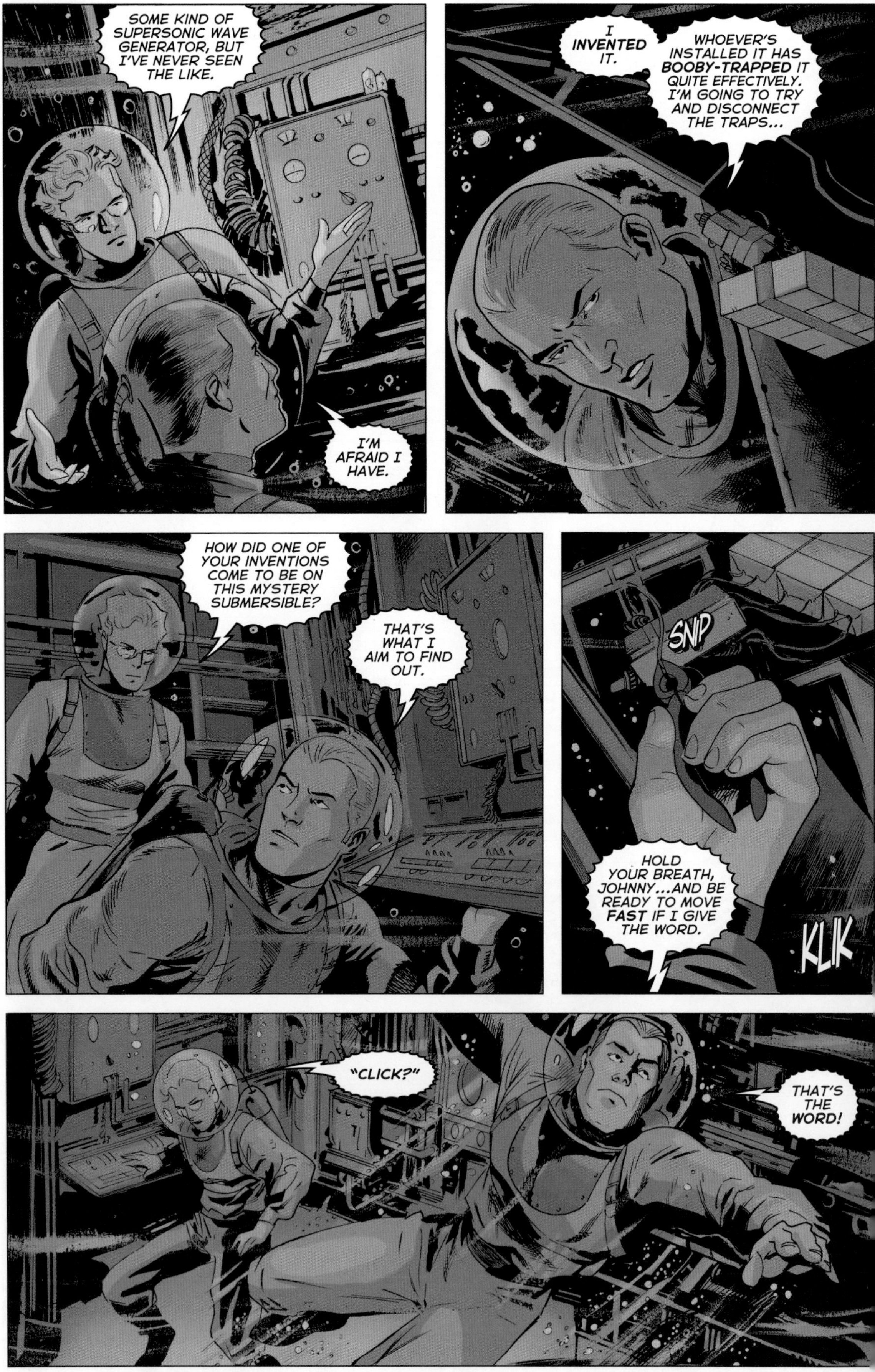
SOME KIND OF SUPERSONIC WAVE GENERATOR, BUT I'VE NEVER SEEN THE LIKE.
I'M AFRAID I HAVE.
I INVENTED IT.
WHOEVER'S INSTALLED IT HAS BOOBY-TRAPPED IT QUITE EFFECTIVELY. I'M GOING TO TRY AND DISCONNECT THE TRAPS...
HOW DID ONE OF YOUR INVENTIONS COME TO BE ON THIS MYSTERY SUBMERSIBLE?
THAT'S WHAT I AIM TO FIND OUT.
SNIP
HOLD YOUR BREATH, JOHNNY...AND BE READY TO MOVE FAST IF I GIVE THE WORD.
KLIK
"CLICK?"
THAT'S THE WORD!

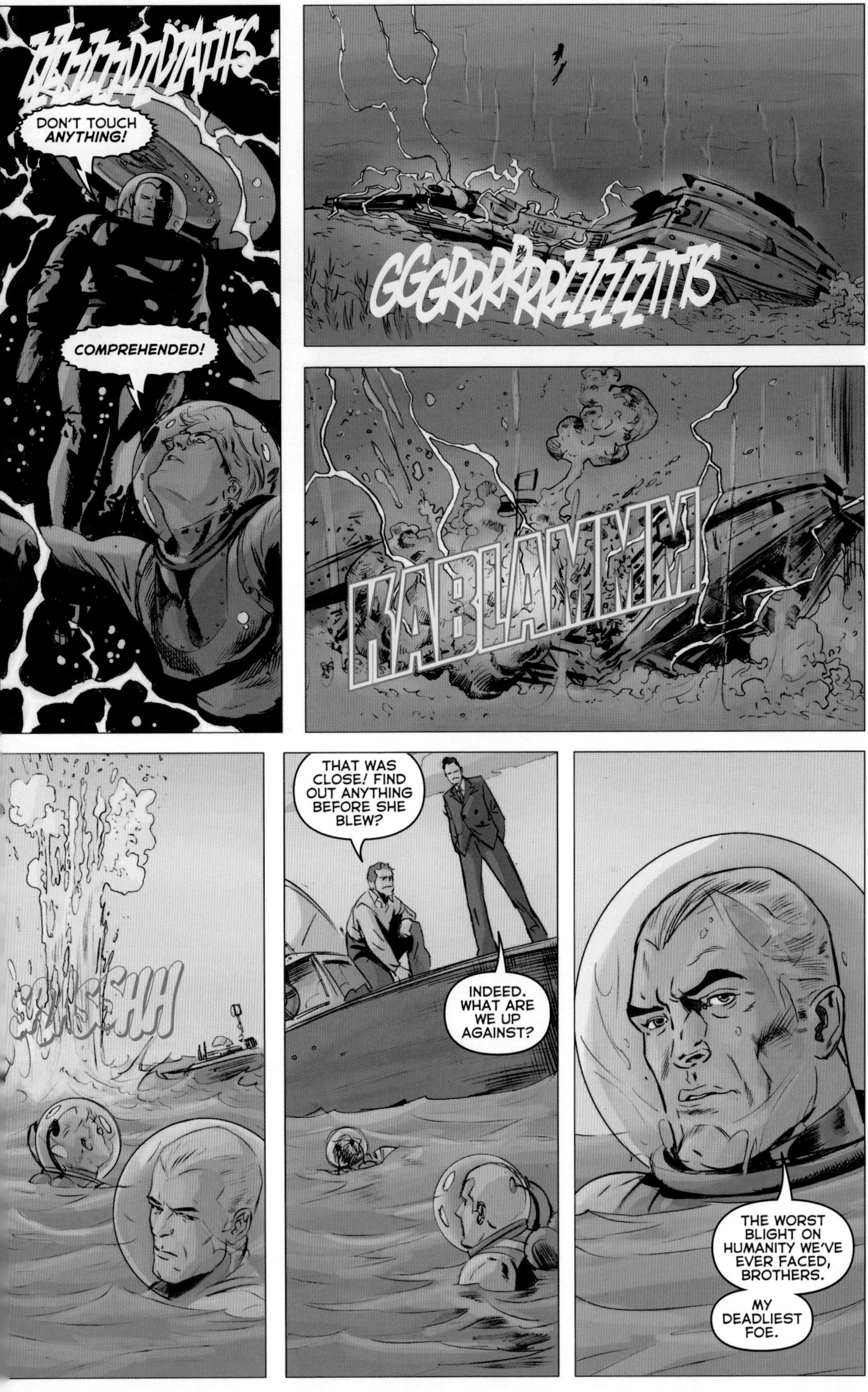
ZZZZZZZZZDZDZATTTS
DON'T TOUCH ANYTHING!
COMPREHENDED!
GGGRRRRRRRZZZZZZZTTTS
KABLAMMM
SPLASHH
THAT WAS CLOSE! FIND OUT ANYTHING BEFORE SHE BLEW?
INDEED. WHAT ARE WE UP AGAINST?
THE WORST BLIGHT ON HUMANITY WE'VE EVER FACED, BROTHERS.
MY DEADLIEST FOE.

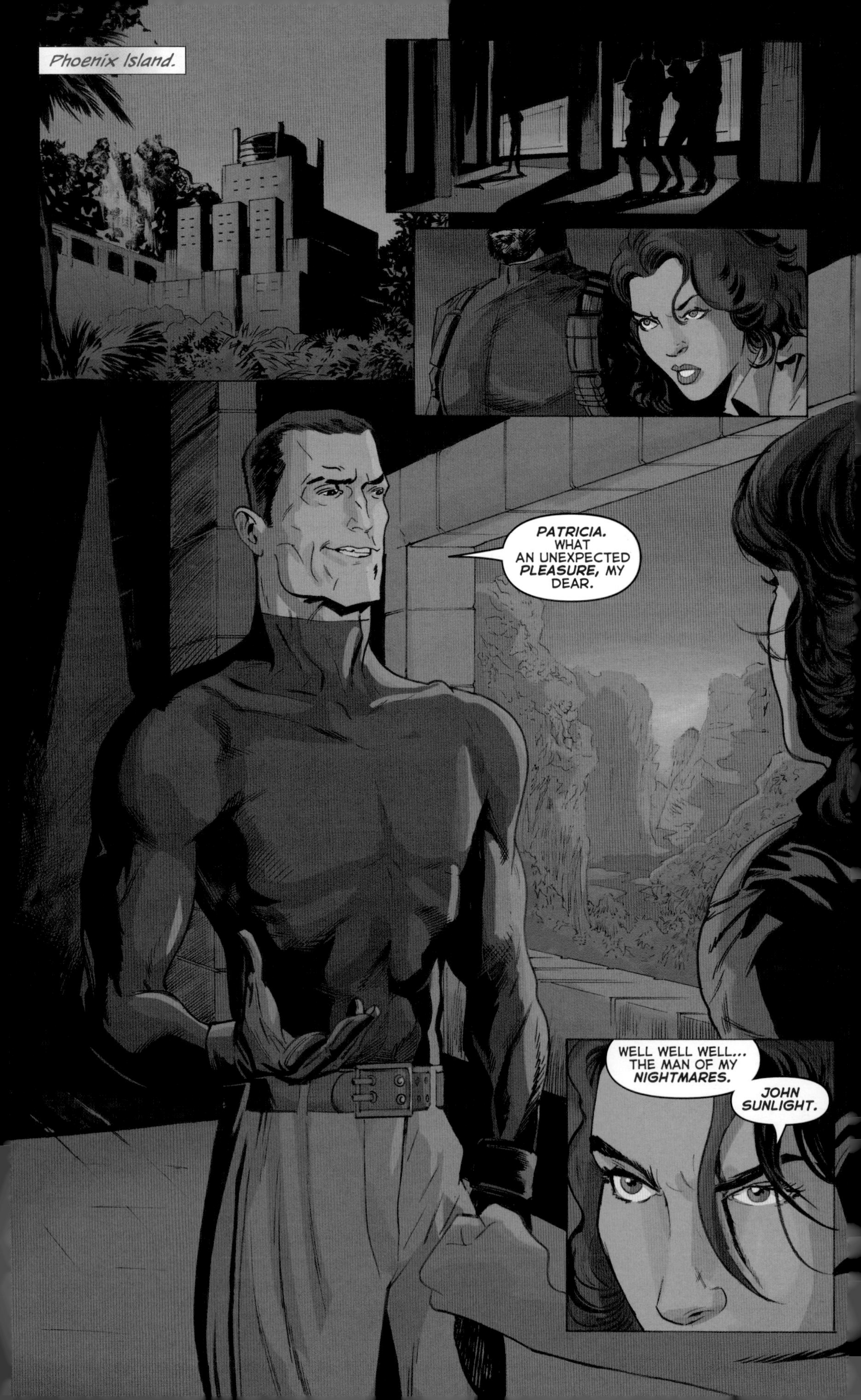
Phoenix Island.
PATRICIA. WHAT AN UNEXPECTED PLEASURE, MY DEAR.
WELL WELL WELL... THE MAN OF MY NIGHTMARES.
JOHN SUNLIGHT.

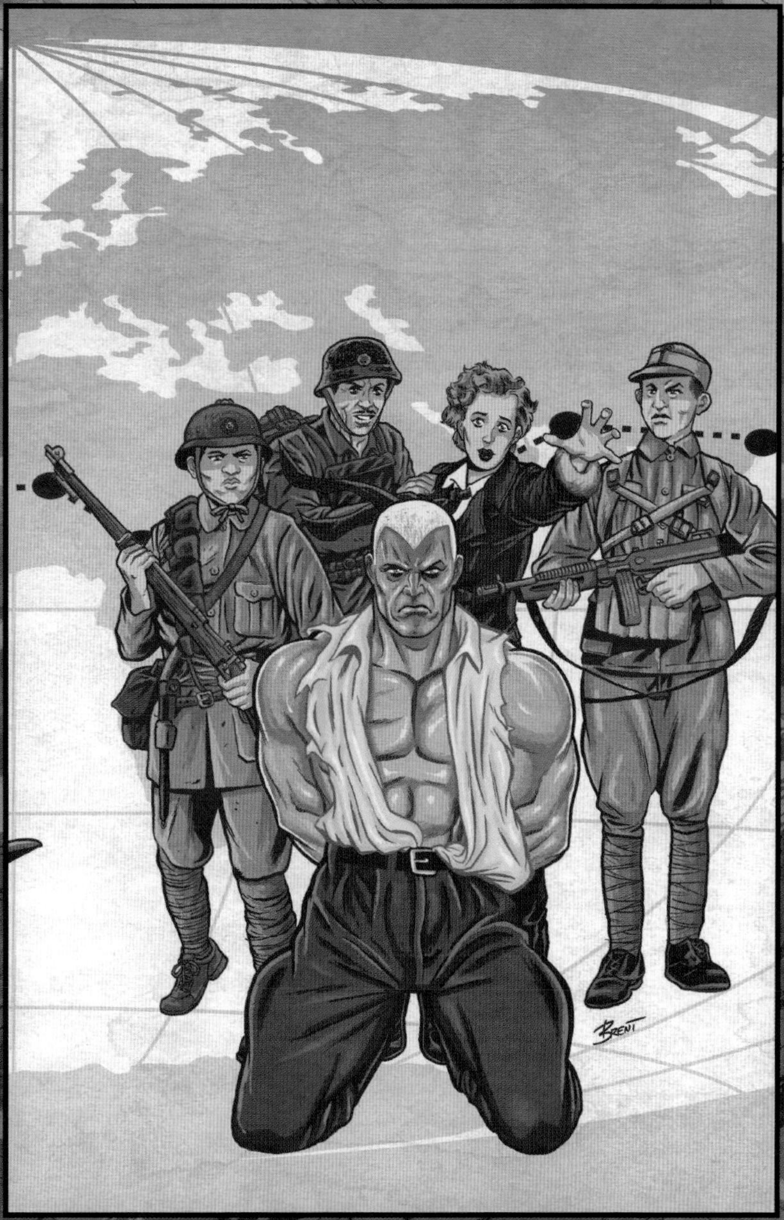
BRENT

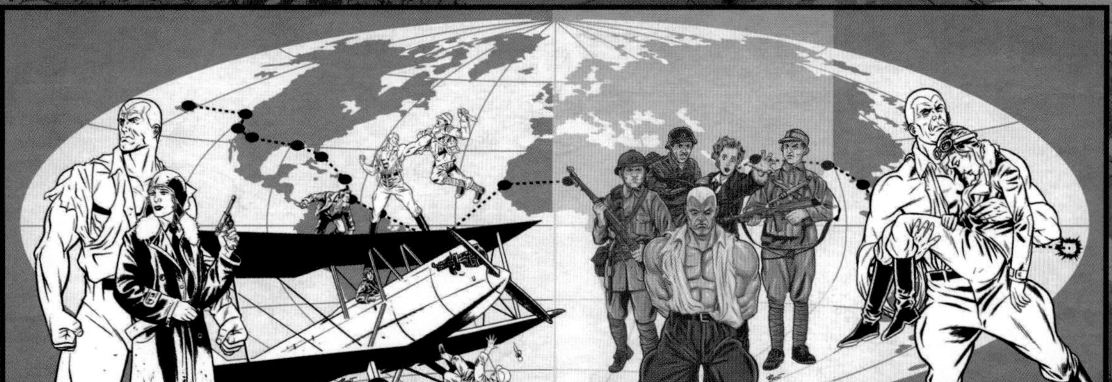

ISSUE THREE CONNECTING COVER ART BY BRENT SCHOONOVER

THREE

"RISING SUNLIGHT"

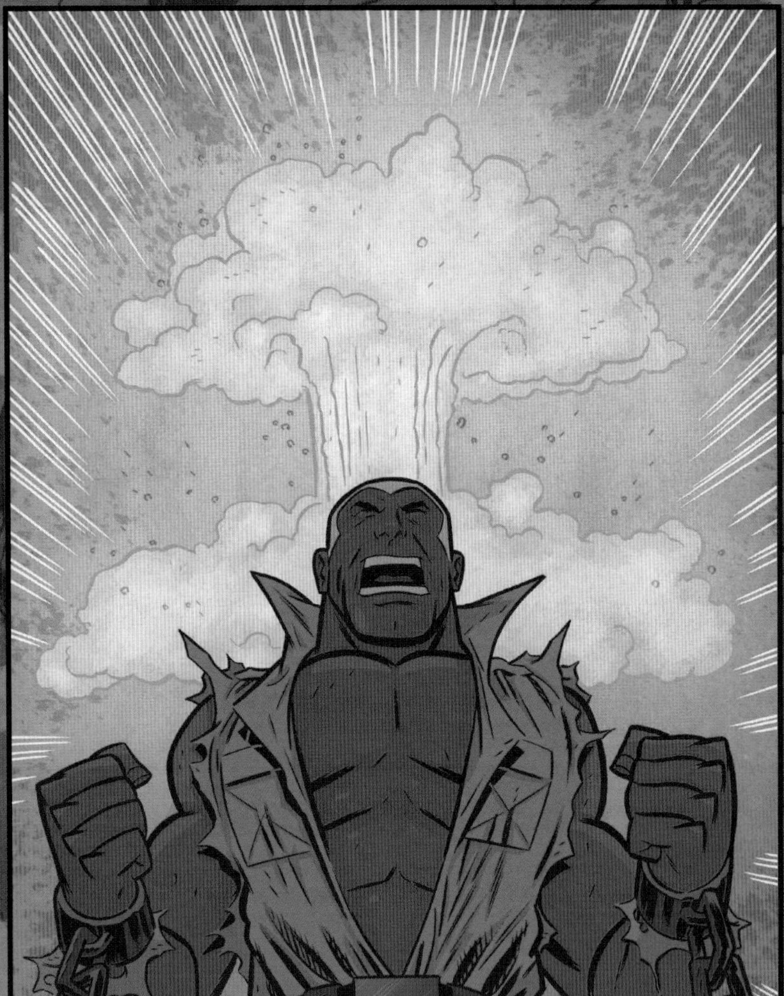

ISSUE THREE VARIANT COVER ART BY ANTHONY MARQUES
INKS BY J. BONE, COLORS BY CHRIS O'HALLORAN

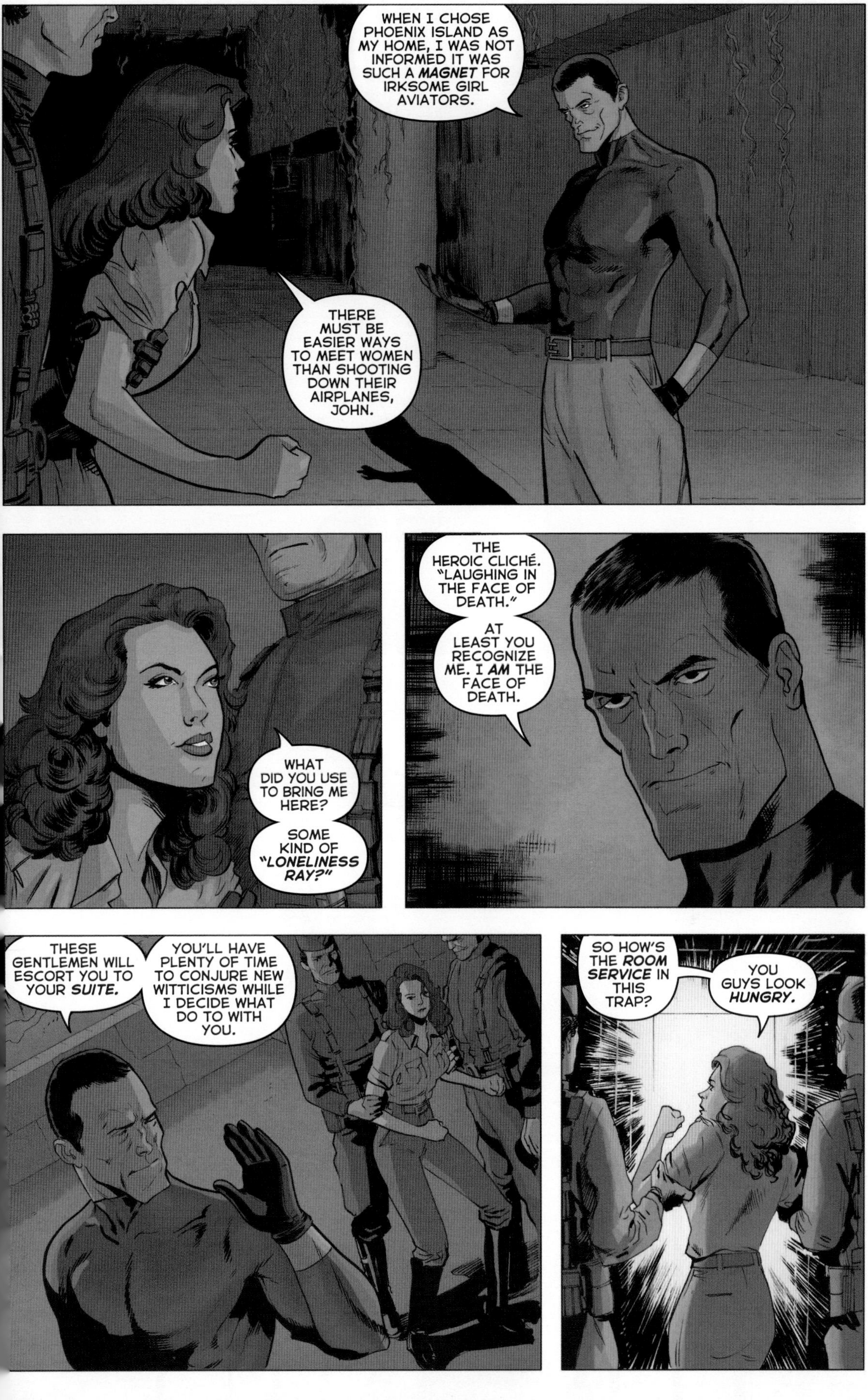
WHEN I CHOSE PHOENIX ISLAND AS MY HOME, I WAS NOT INFORMED IT WAS SUCH A MAGNET FOR IRKSOME GIRL AVIATORS.
THERE MUST BE EASIER WAYS TO MEET WOMEN THAN SHOOTING DOWN THEIR AIRPLANES, JOHN.
WHAT DID YOU USE TO BRING ME HERE?
SOME KIND OF "LONELINESS RAY?"
THE HEROIC CLICHÉ. "LAUGHING IN THE FACE OF DEATH."
AT LEAST YOU RECOGNIZE ME. I AM THE FACE OF DEATH.
THESE GENTLEMEN WILL ESCORT YOU TO YOUR SUITE.
YOU'LL HAVE PLENTY OF TIME TO CONJURE NEW WITTICISMS WHILE I DECIDE WHAT DO TO WITH YOU.
SO HOW'S THE ROOM SERVICE IN THIS TRAP?
YOU GUYS LOOK HUNGRY.

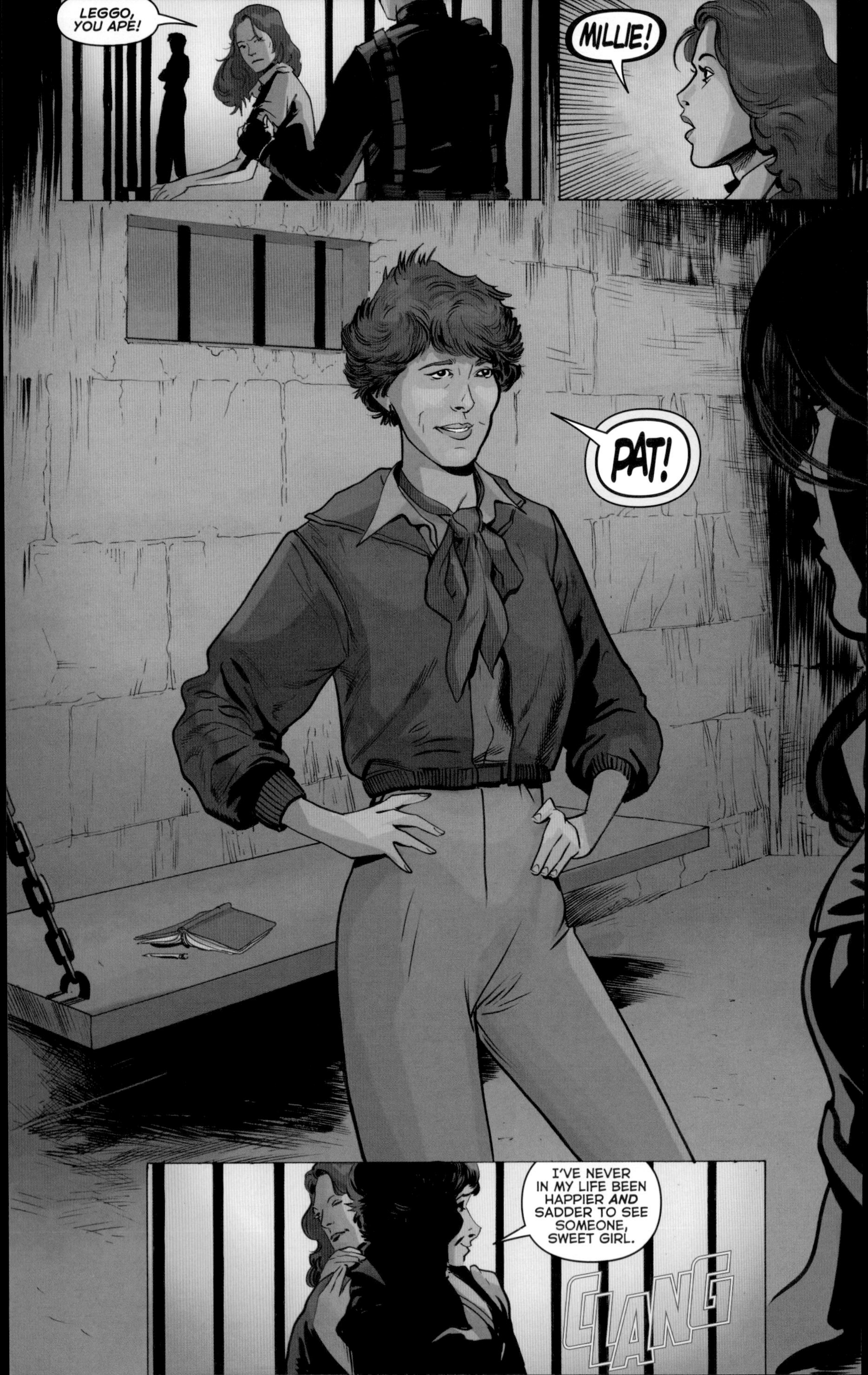
LEGGO, YOU APE!
MILLIE!
PAT!
I'VE NEVER IN MY LIFE BEEN HAPPIER AND SADDER TO SEE SOMEONE, SWEET GIRL.
CLANG

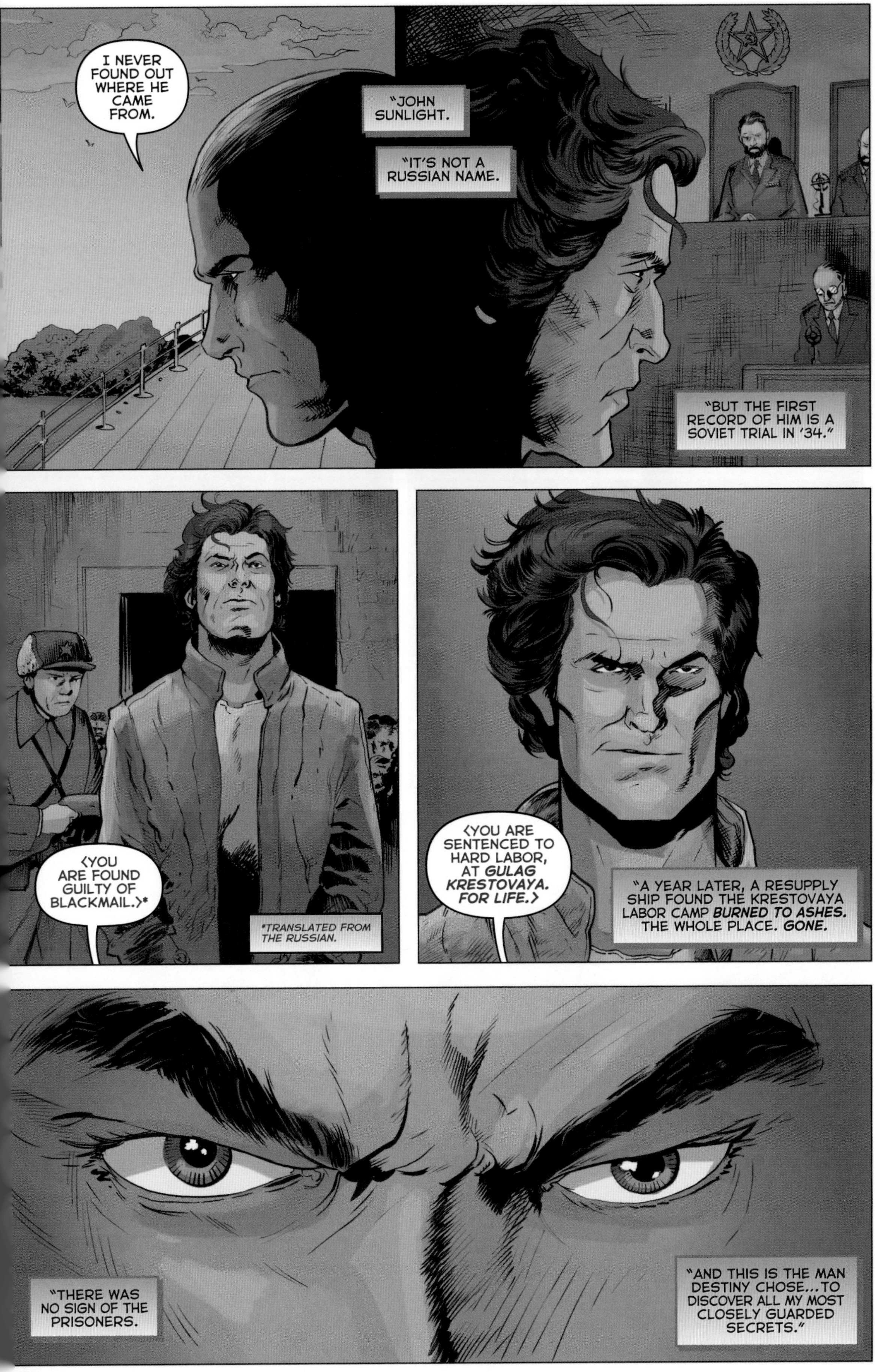
I NEVER FOUND OUT WHERE HE CAME FROM.
"JOHN SUNLIGHT.
"IT'S NOT A RUSSIAN NAME.
"BUT THE FIRST RECORD OF HIM IS A SOVIET TRIAL IN '34."
‹YOU ARE FOUND GUILTY OF BLACKMAIL.›*
*TRANSLATED FROM THE RUSSIAN.
‹YOU ARE SENTENCED TO HARD LABOR, AT GULAG KRESTOVAYA. FOR LIFE.›
"A YEAR LATER, A RESUPPLY SHIP FOUND THE KRESTOVAYA LABOR CAMP BURNED TO ASHES. THE WHOLE PLACE. GONE.
"THERE WAS NO SIGN OF THE PRISONERS.
"AND THIS IS THE MAN DESTINY CHOSE...TO DISCOVER ALL MY MOST CLOSELY GUARDED SECRETS."

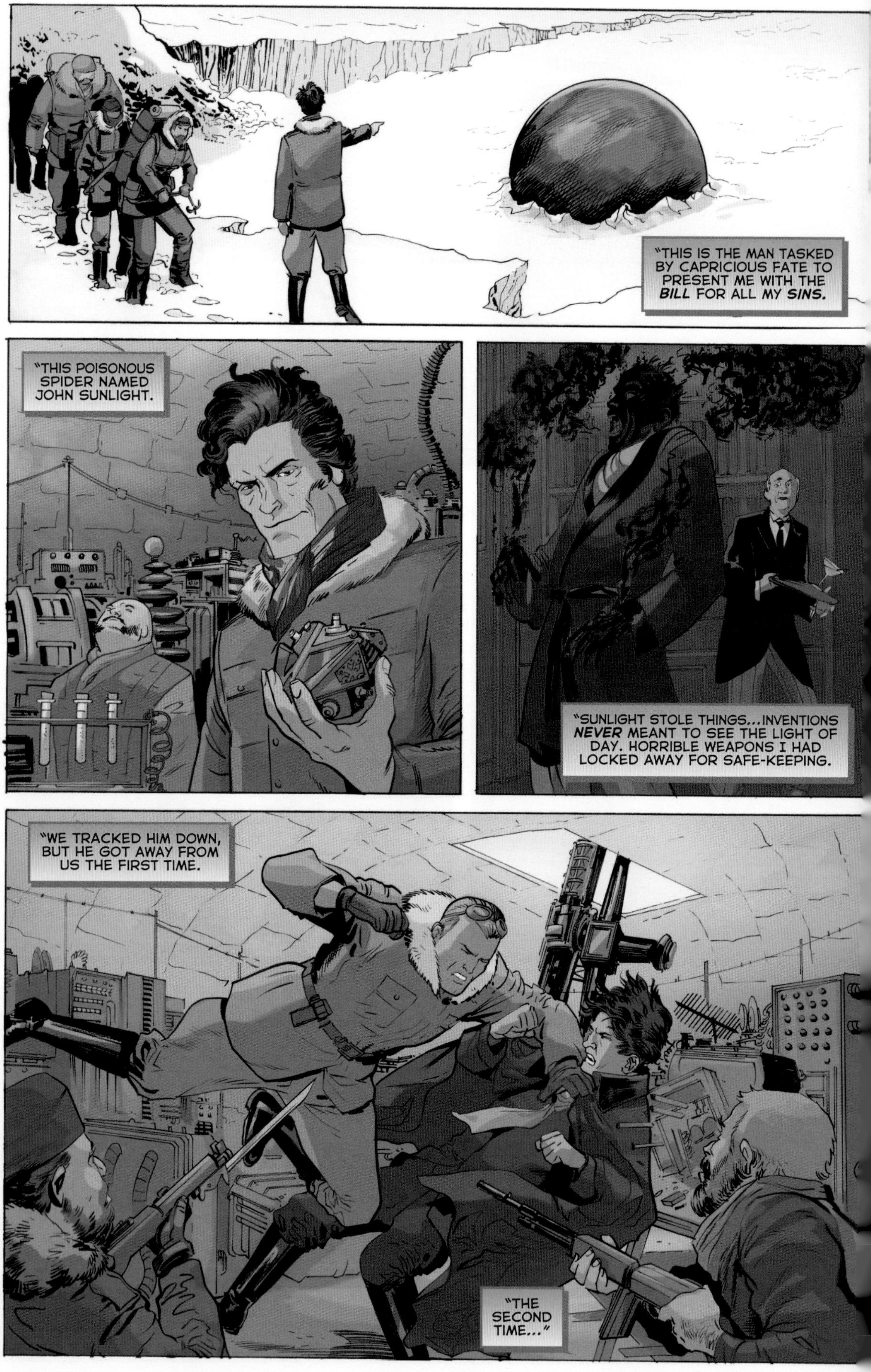
"THIS IS THE MAN TASKED BY CAPRICIOUS FATE TO PRESENT ME WITH THE *BILL* FOR ALL MY *SINS*.
"THIS POISONOUS SPIDER NAMED JOHN SUNLIGHT.
"SUNLIGHT STOLE THINGS...INVENTIONS *NEVER* MEANT TO SEE THE LIGHT OF DAY. HORRIBLE WEAPONS I HAD LOCKED AWAY FOR SAFE-KEEPING.
"WE TRACKED HIM DOWN, BUT HE GOT AWAY FROM US THE FIRST TIME.
"THE SECOND TIME..."

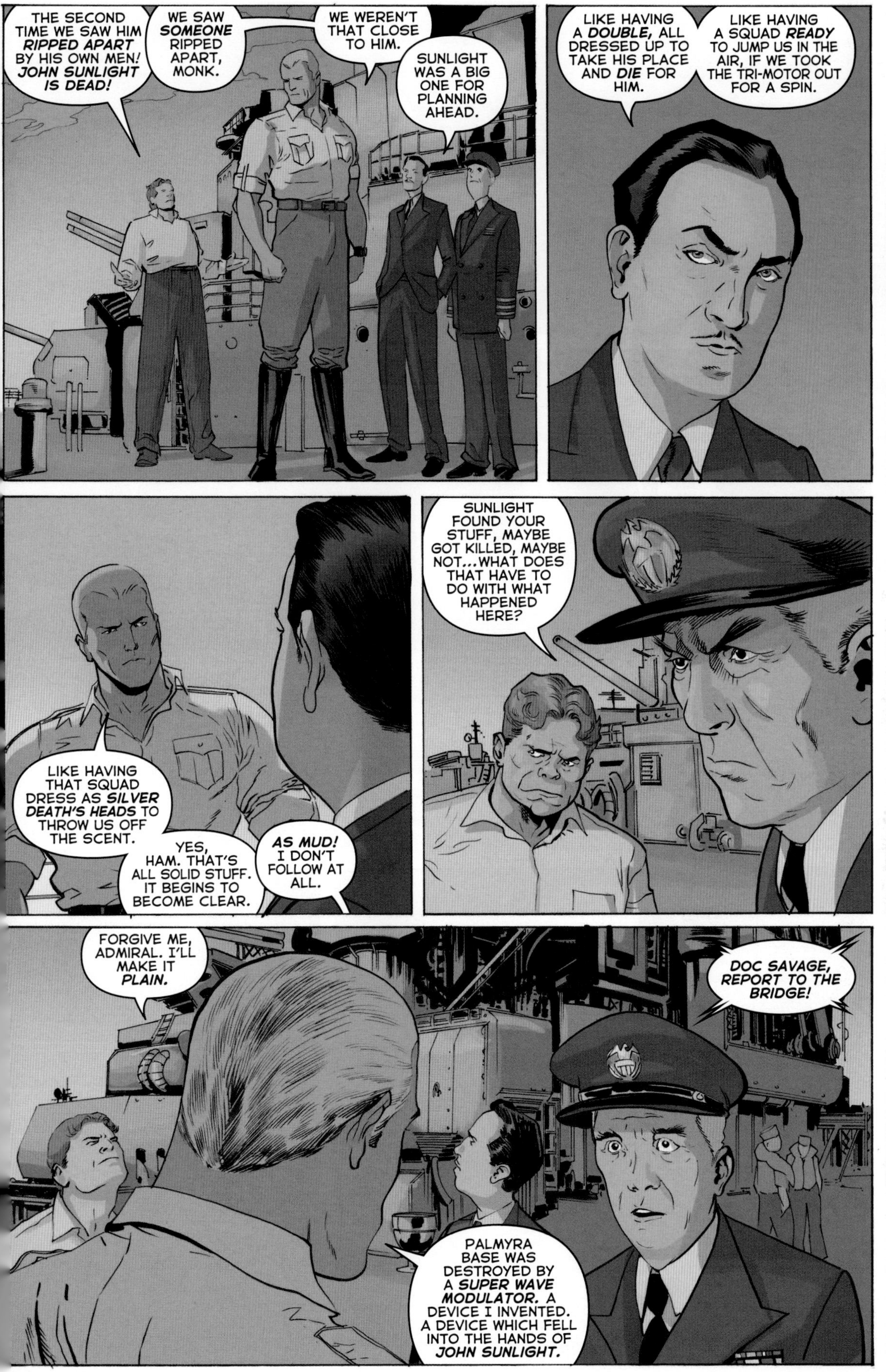
THE SECOND TIME WE SAW HIM RIPPED APART BY HIS OWN MEN! JOHN SUNLIGHT IS DEAD!
WE SAW SOMEONE RIPPED APART, MONK.
WE WEREN'T THAT CLOSE TO HIM.
SUNLIGHT WAS A BIG ONE FOR PLANNING AHEAD.
LIKE HAVING A DOUBLE, ALL DRESSED UP TO TAKE HIS PLACE AND DIE FOR HIM.
LIKE HAVING A SQUAD READY TO JUMP US IN THE AIR, IF WE TOOK THE TRI-MOTOR OUT FOR A SPIN.
LIKE HAVING THAT SQUAD DRESS AS SILVER DEATH'S HEADS TO THROW US OFF THE SCENT.
YES, HAM. THAT'S ALL SOLID STUFF. IT BEGINS TO BECOME CLEAR.
AS MUD! I DON'T FOLLOW AT ALL.
SUNLIGHT FOUND YOUR STUFF, MAYBE GOT KILLED, MAYBE NOT...WHAT DOES THAT HAVE TO DO WITH WHAT HAPPENED HERE?
FORGIVE ME, ADMIRAL. I'LL MAKE IT PLAIN.
DOC SAVAGE, REPORT TO THE BRIDGE!
PALMYRA BASE WAS DESTROYED BY A SUPER WAVE MODULATOR. A DEVICE I INVENTED. A DEVICE WHICH FELL INTO THE HANDS OF JOHN SUNLIGHT.

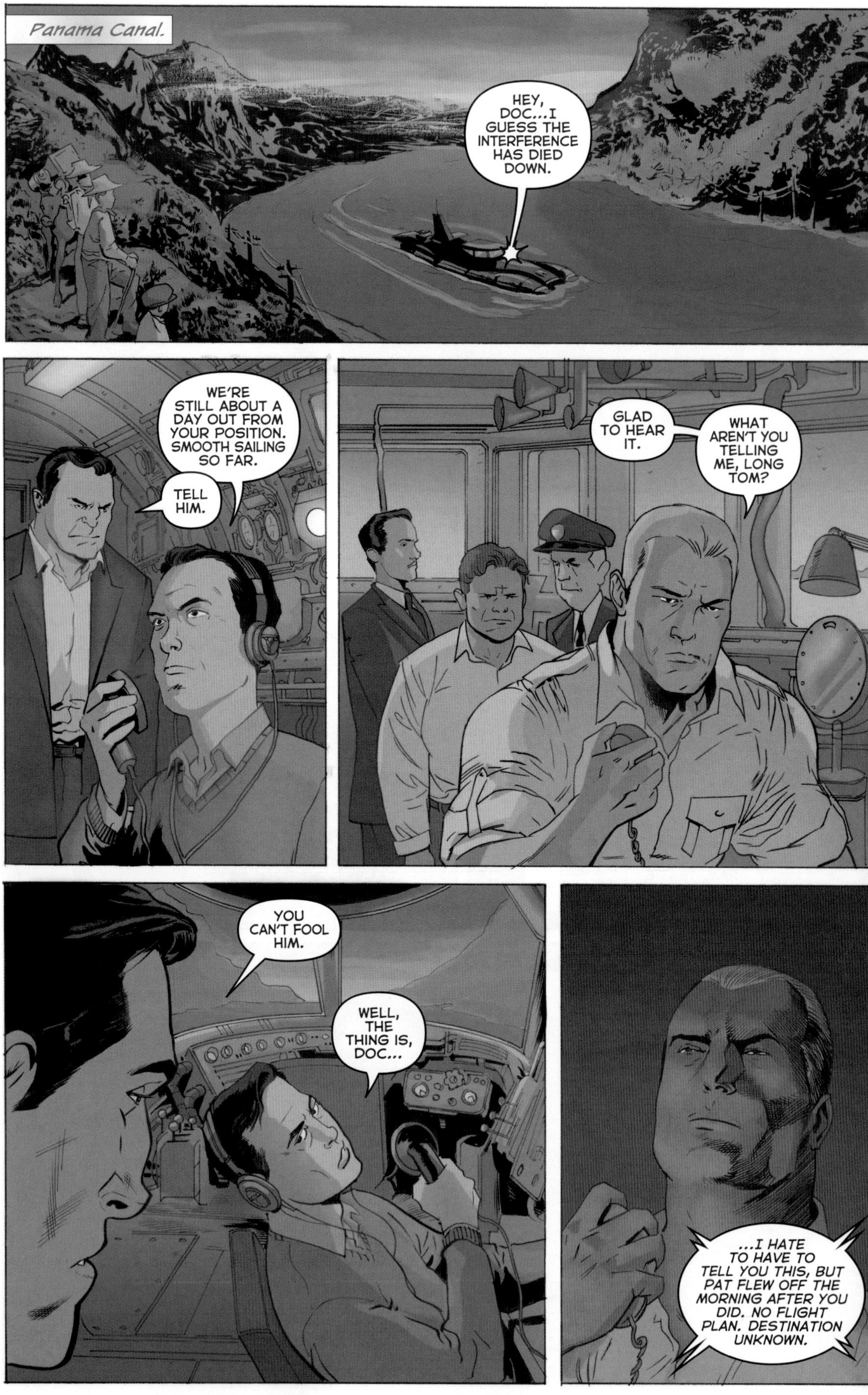
Panama Canal.
HEY, DOC...I GUESS THE INTERFERENCE HAS DIED DOWN.
WE'RE STILL ABOUT A DAY OUT FROM YOUR POSITION. SMOOTH SAILING SO FAR.
TELL HIM.
GLAD TO HEAR IT.
WHAT AREN'T YOU TELLING ME, LONG TOM?
YOU CAN'T FOOL HIM.
WELL, THE THING IS, DOC...
...I HATE TO HAVE TO TELL YOU THIS, BUT PAT FLEW OFF THE MORNING AFTER YOU DID. NO FLIGHT PLAN. DESTINATION UNKNOWN.

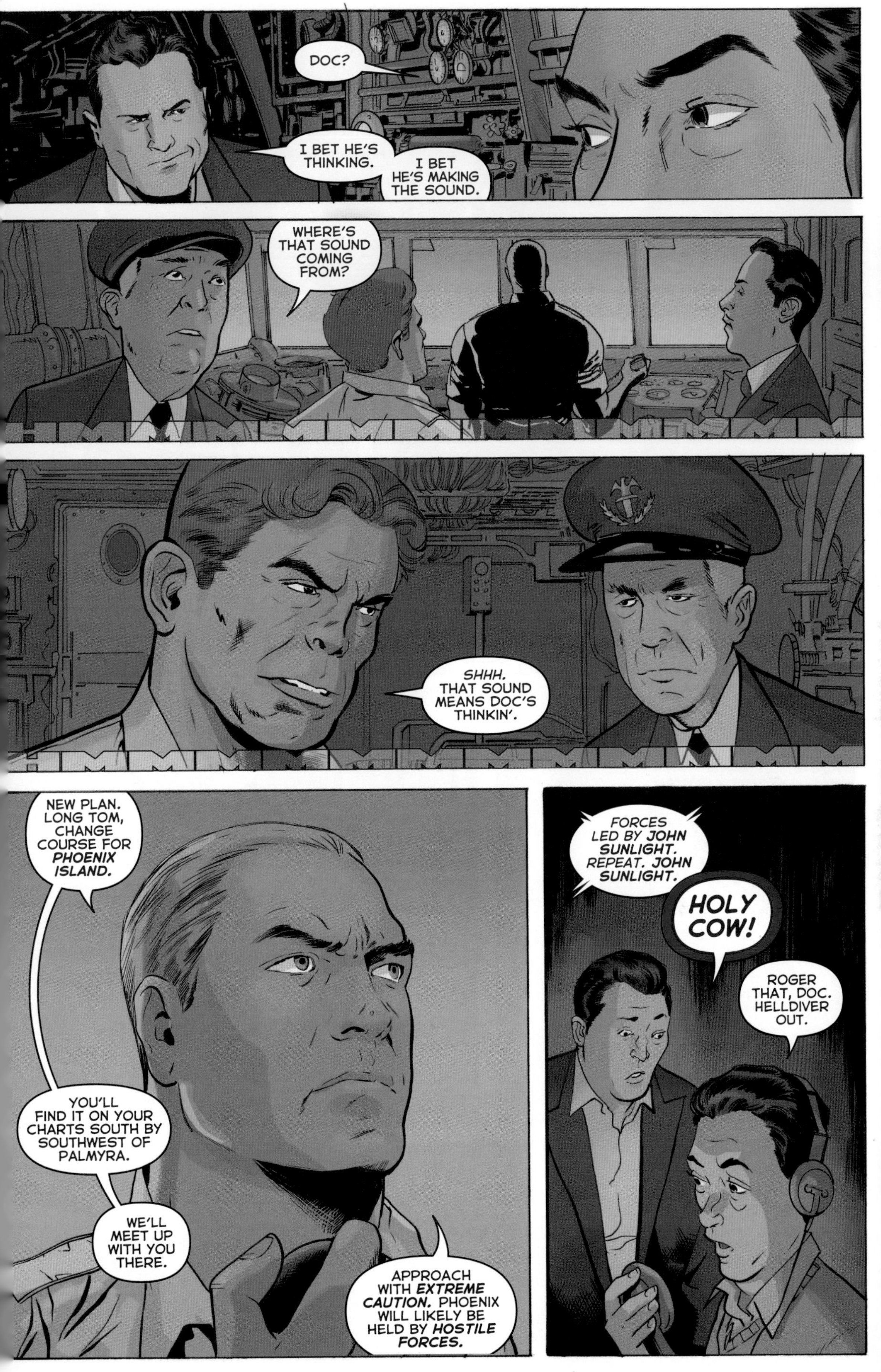
DOC?
I BET HE'S THINKING.
I BET HE'S MAKING THE SOUND.
WHERE'S THAT SOUND COMING FROM?
HMMMMMMMMMMM
SHHH. THAT SOUND MEANS DOC'S THINKIN'.
HMMMMMMMMMMM
NEW PLAN. LONG TOM, CHANGE COURSE FOR *PHOENIX ISLAND.*
YOU'LL FIND IT ON YOUR CHARTS SOUTH BY SOUTHWEST OF PALMYRA.
WE'LL MEET UP WITH YOU THERE.
APPROACH WITH *EXTREME CAUTION.* PHOENIX WILL LIKELY BE HELD BY *HOSTILE FORCES.*
FORCES LED BY **JOHN SUNLIGHT**. REPEAT. **JOHN SUNLIGHT**.
HOLY COW!
ROGER THAT, DOC. HELLDIVER OUT.

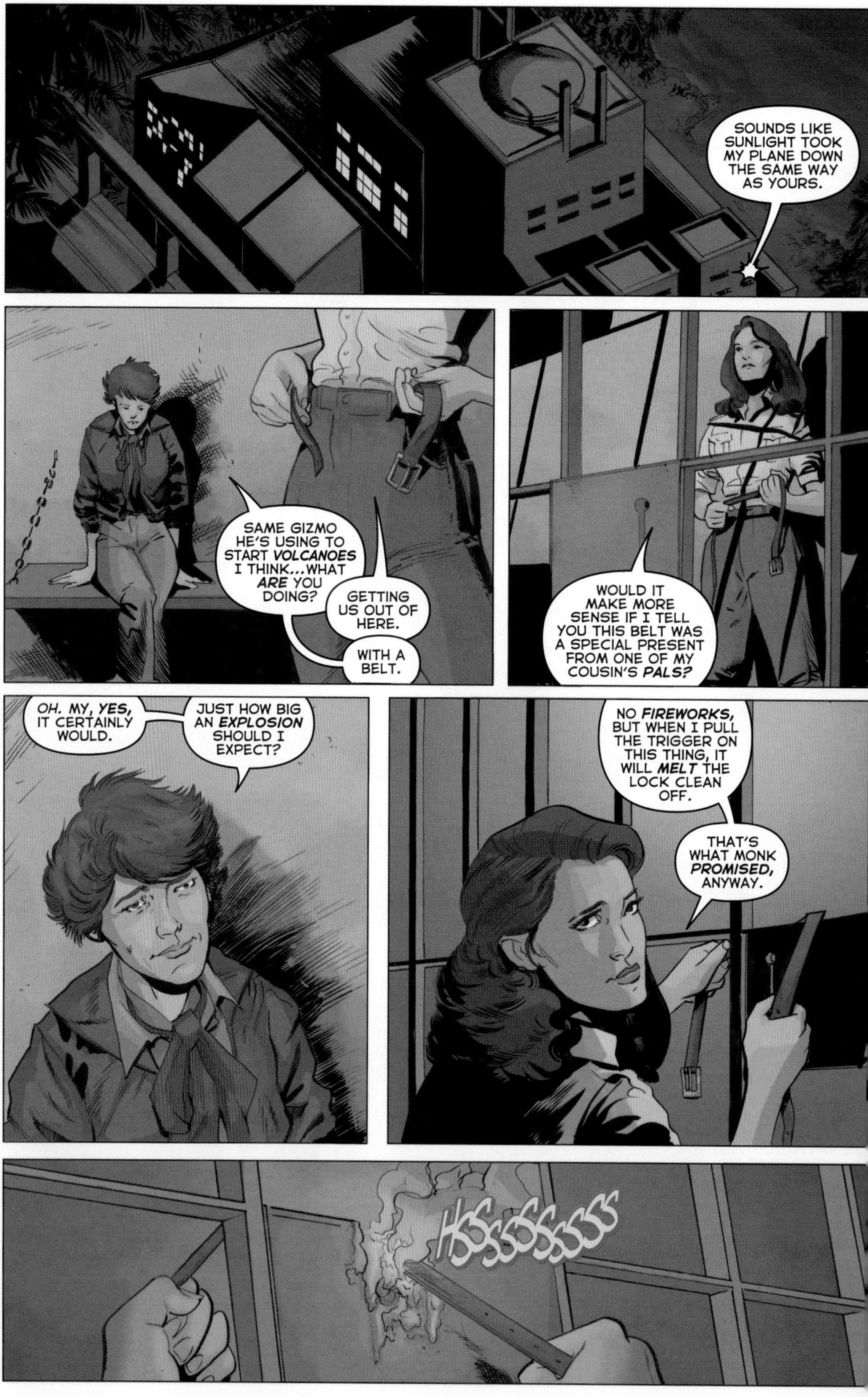
SOUNDS LIKE SUNLIGHT TOOK MY PLANE DOWN THE SAME WAY AS YOURS.
SAME GIZMO HE'S USING TO START VOLCANOES I THINK...WHAT ARE YOU DOING?
GETTING US OUT OF HERE.
WITH A BELT.
WOULD IT MAKE MORE SENSE IF I TELL YOU THIS BELT WAS A SPECIAL PRESENT FROM ONE OF MY COUSIN'S PALS?
OH. MY, YES, IT CERTAINLY WOULD.
JUST HOW BIG AN EXPLOSION SHOULD I EXPECT?
NO FIREWORKS, BUT WHEN I PULL THE TRIGGER ON THIS THING, IT WILL MELT THE LOCK CLEAN OFF.
THAT'S WHAT MONK PROMISED, ANYWAY.
HSSSSSSSSSS

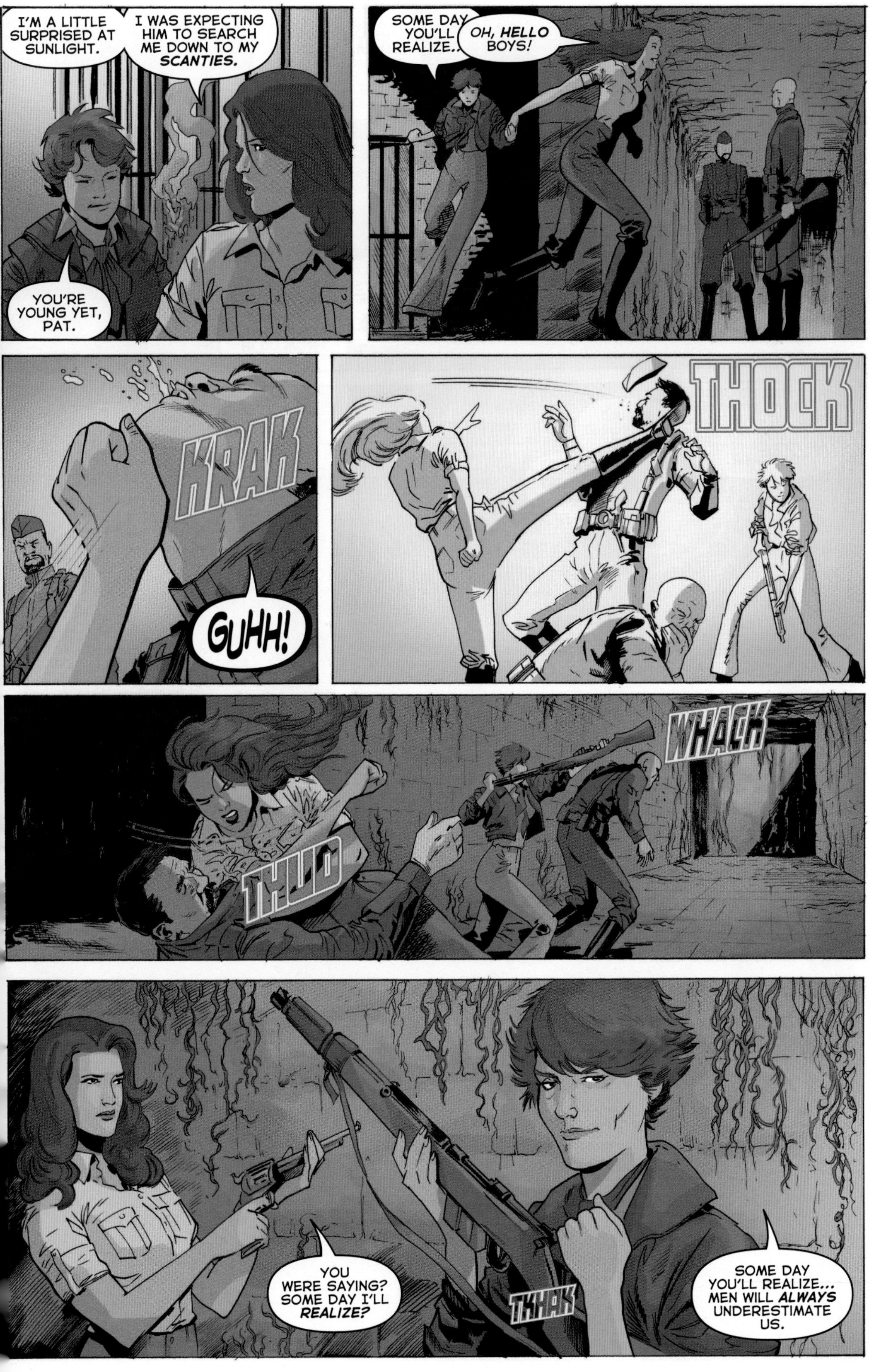

I'M A LITTLE SURPRISED AT SUNLIGHT.
I WAS EXPECTING HIM TO SEARCH ME DOWN TO MY SCANTIES.
YOU'RE YOUNG YET, PAT.
SOME DAY YOU'LL REALIZE...
OH, HELLO BOYS!
KRAK
GUHH!
THOCK
WHACK
THUD
YOU WERE SAYING? SOME DAY I'LL REALIZE?
TKHAK
SOME DAY YOU'LL REALIZE... MEN WILL ALWAYS UNDERESTIMATE US.

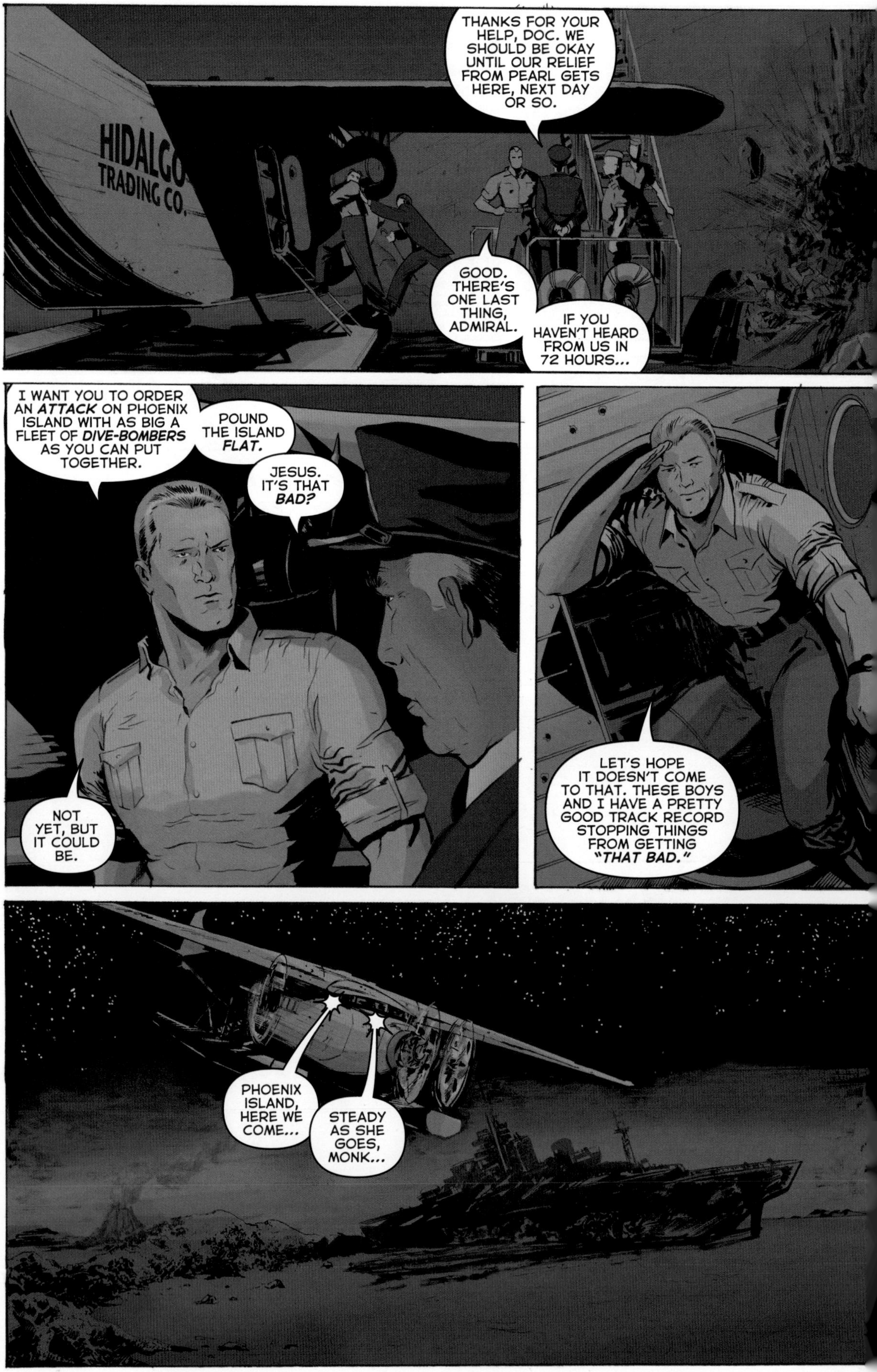
HIDALGO TRADING CO.
THANKS FOR YOUR HELP, DOC. WE SHOULD BE OKAY UNTIL OUR RELIEF FROM PEARL GETS HERE, NEXT DAY OR SO.
GOOD. THERE'S ONE LAST THING, ADMIRAL.
IF YOU HAVEN'T HEARD FROM US IN 72 HOURS...
I WANT YOU TO ORDER AN ATTACK ON PHOENIX ISLAND WITH AS BIG A FLEET OF DIVE-BOMBERS AS YOU CAN PUT TOGETHER.
POUND THE ISLAND FLAT.
JESUS. IT'S THAT BAD?
NOT YET, BUT IT COULD BE.
LET'S HOPE IT DOESN'T COME TO THAT. THESE BOYS AND I HAVE A PRETTY GOOD TRACK RECORD STOPPING THINGS FROM GETTING "THAT BAD."
PHOENIX ISLAND, HERE WE COME...
STEADY AS SHE GOES, MONK...

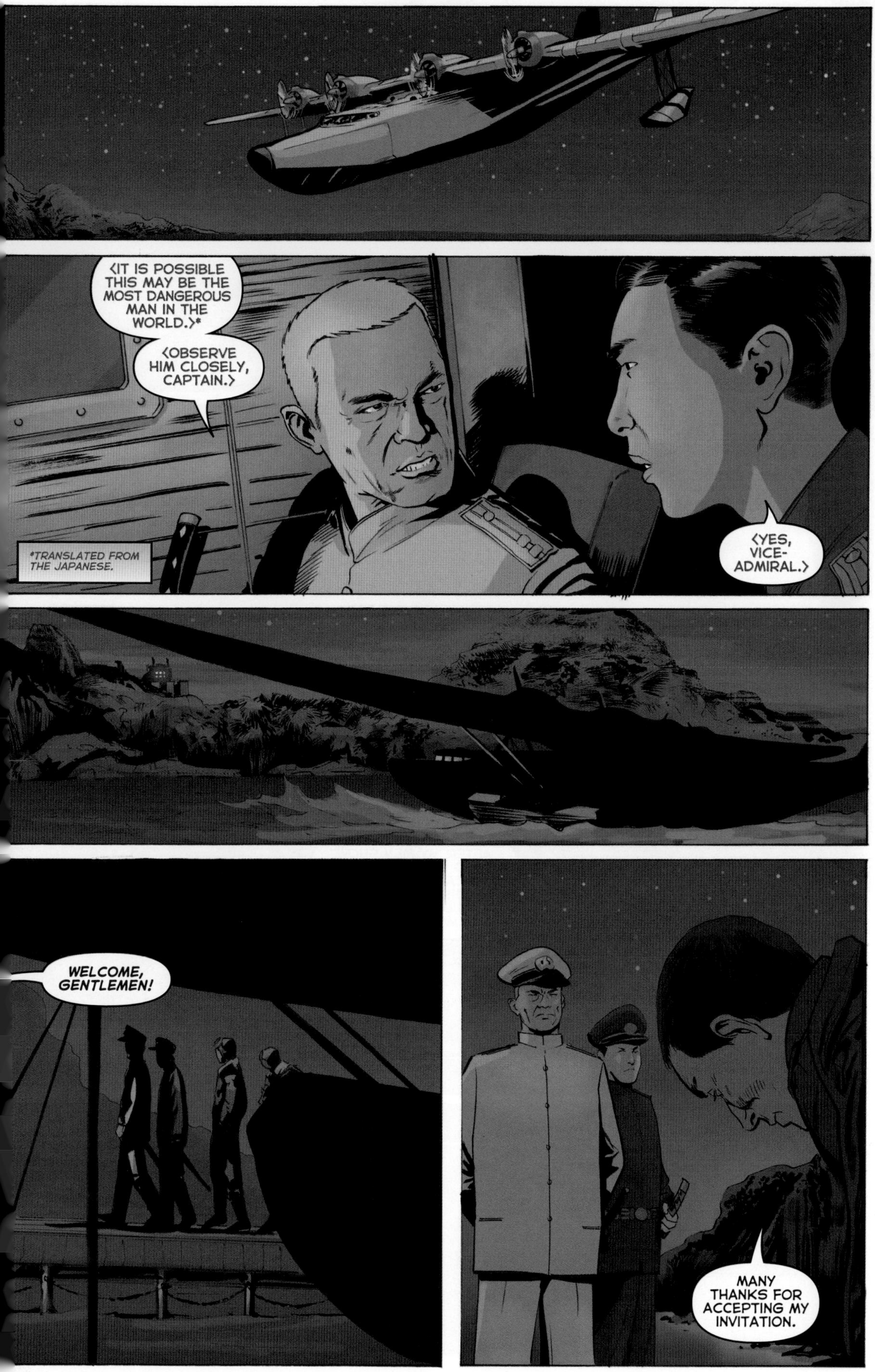

<IT IS POSSIBLE THIS MAY BE THE MOST DANGEROUS MAN IN THE WORLD.>*
<OBSERVE HIM CLOSELY, CAPTAIN.>
*TRANSLATED FROM THE JAPANESE.
<YES, VICE-ADMIRAL.>
WELCOME, GENTLEMEN!
MANY THANKS FOR ACCEPTING MY INVITATION.

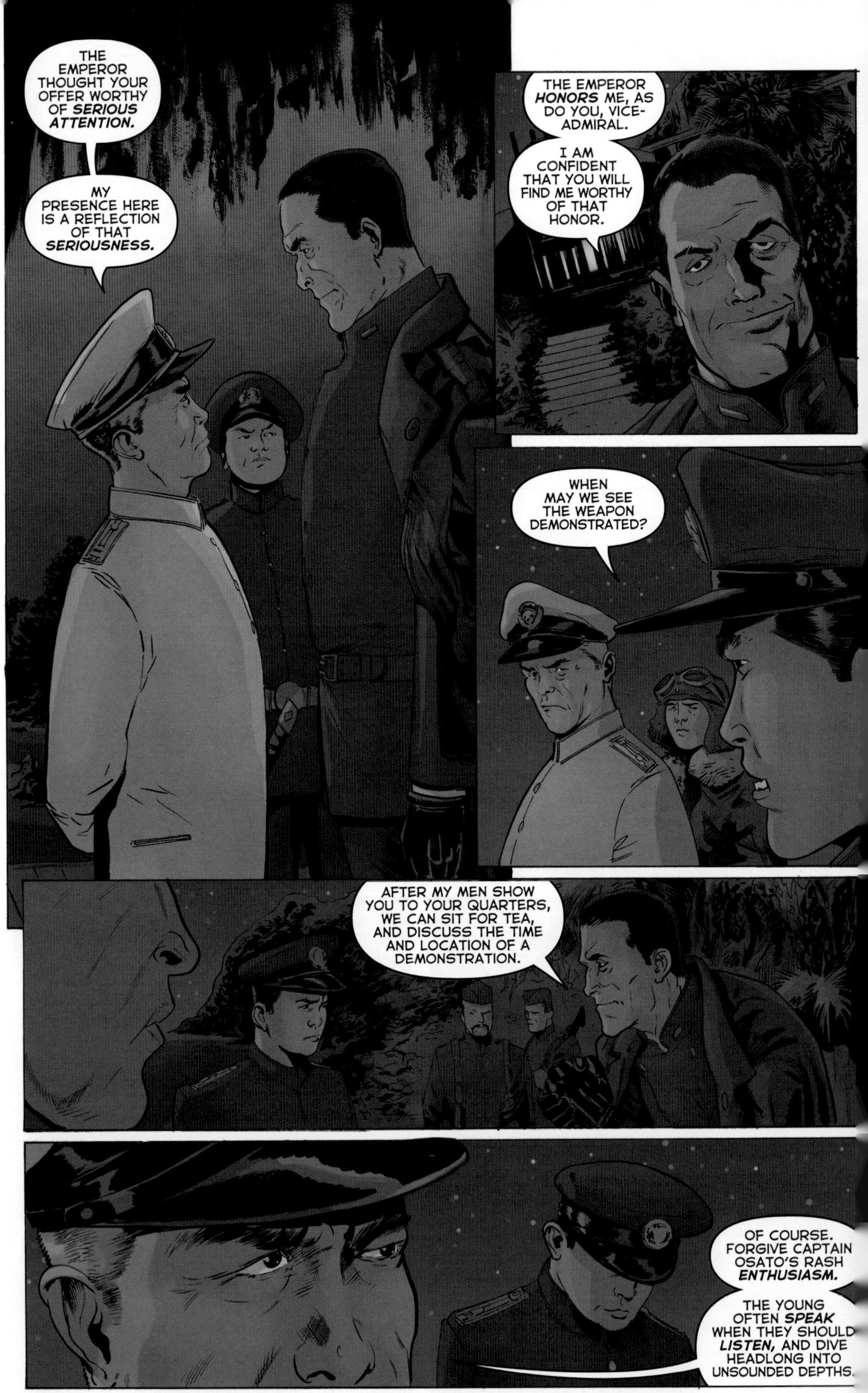
THE EMPEROR THOUGHT YOUR OFFER WORTHY OF *SERIOUS ATTENTION.*
MY PRESENCE HERE IS A REFLECTION OF THAT *SERIOUSNESS.*
THE EMPEROR *HONORS* ME, AS DO YOU, VICE-ADMIRAL.
I AM CONFIDENT THAT YOU WILL FIND ME WORTHY OF THAT HONOR.
WHEN MAY WE SEE THE WEAPON DEMONSTRATED?
AFTER MY MEN SHOW YOU TO YOUR QUARTERS, WE CAN SIT FOR TEA, AND DISCUSS THE TIME AND LOCATION OF A DEMONSTRATION.
OF COURSE. FORGIVE CAPTAIN OSATO'S RASH *ENTHUSIASM.*
THE YOUNG OFTEN *SPEAK* WHEN THEY SHOULD *LISTEN,* AND DIVE HEADLONG INTO UNSOUNDED DEPTHS.

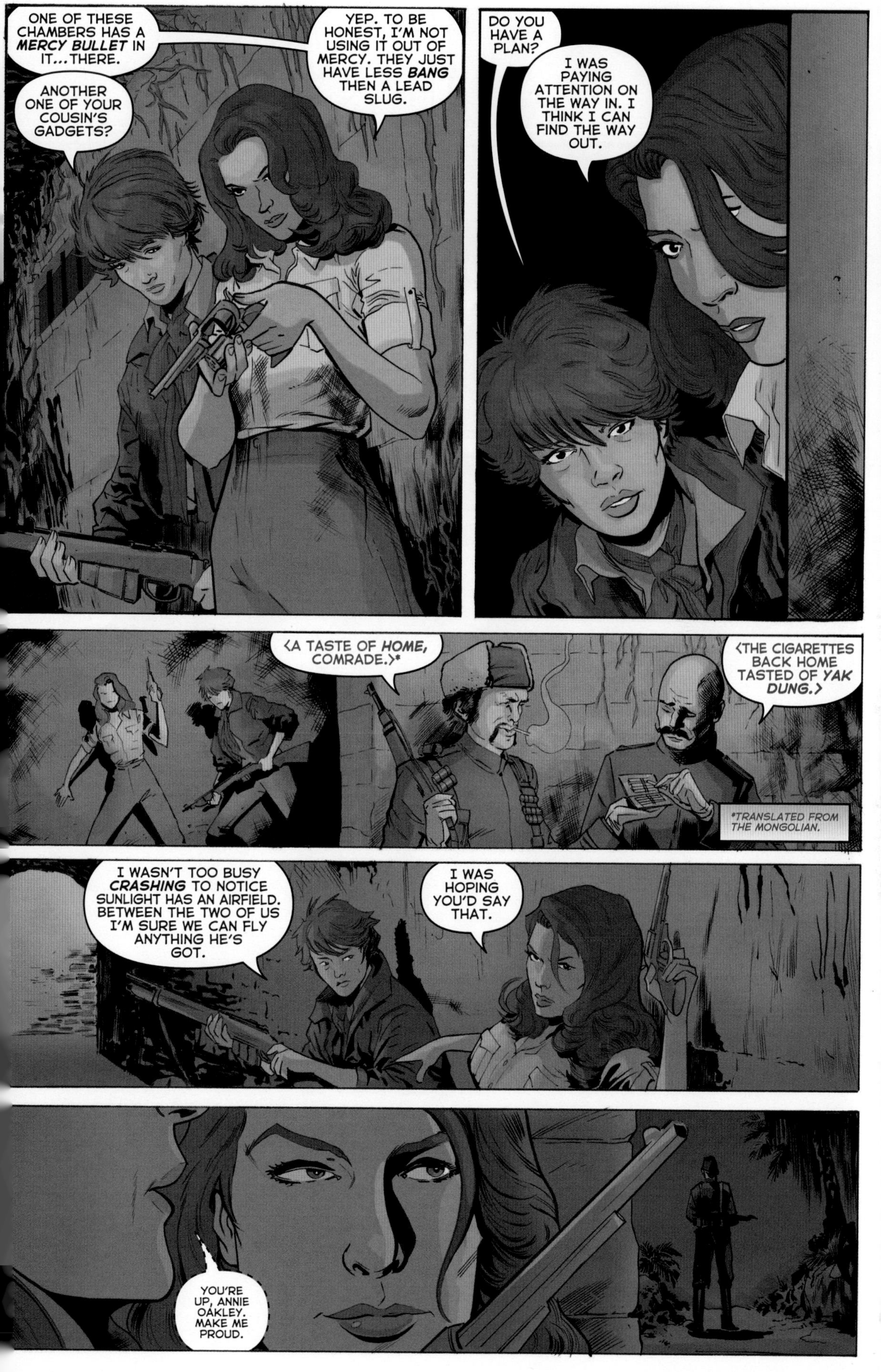
ONE OF THESE CHAMBERS HAS A MERCY BULLET IN IT... THERE.
ANOTHER ONE OF YOUR COUSIN'S GADGETS?
YEP. TO BE HONEST, I'M NOT USING IT OUT OF MERCY. THEY JUST HAVE LESS BANG THEN A LEAD SLUG.
DO YOU HAVE A PLAN?
I WAS PAYING ATTENTION ON THE WAY IN. I THINK I CAN FIND THE WAY OUT.
<A TASTE OF HOME, COMRADE.>*
<THE CIGARETTES BACK HOME TASTED OF YAK DUNG.>
*TRANSLATED FROM THE MONGOLIAN.
I WASN'T TOO BUSY CRASHING TO NOTICE SUNLIGHT HAS AN AIRFIELD. BETWEEN THE TWO OF US I'M SURE WE CAN FLY ANYTHING HE'S GOT.
I WAS HOPING YOU'D SAY THAT.
YOU'RE UP, ANNIE OAKLEY. MAKE ME PROUD.

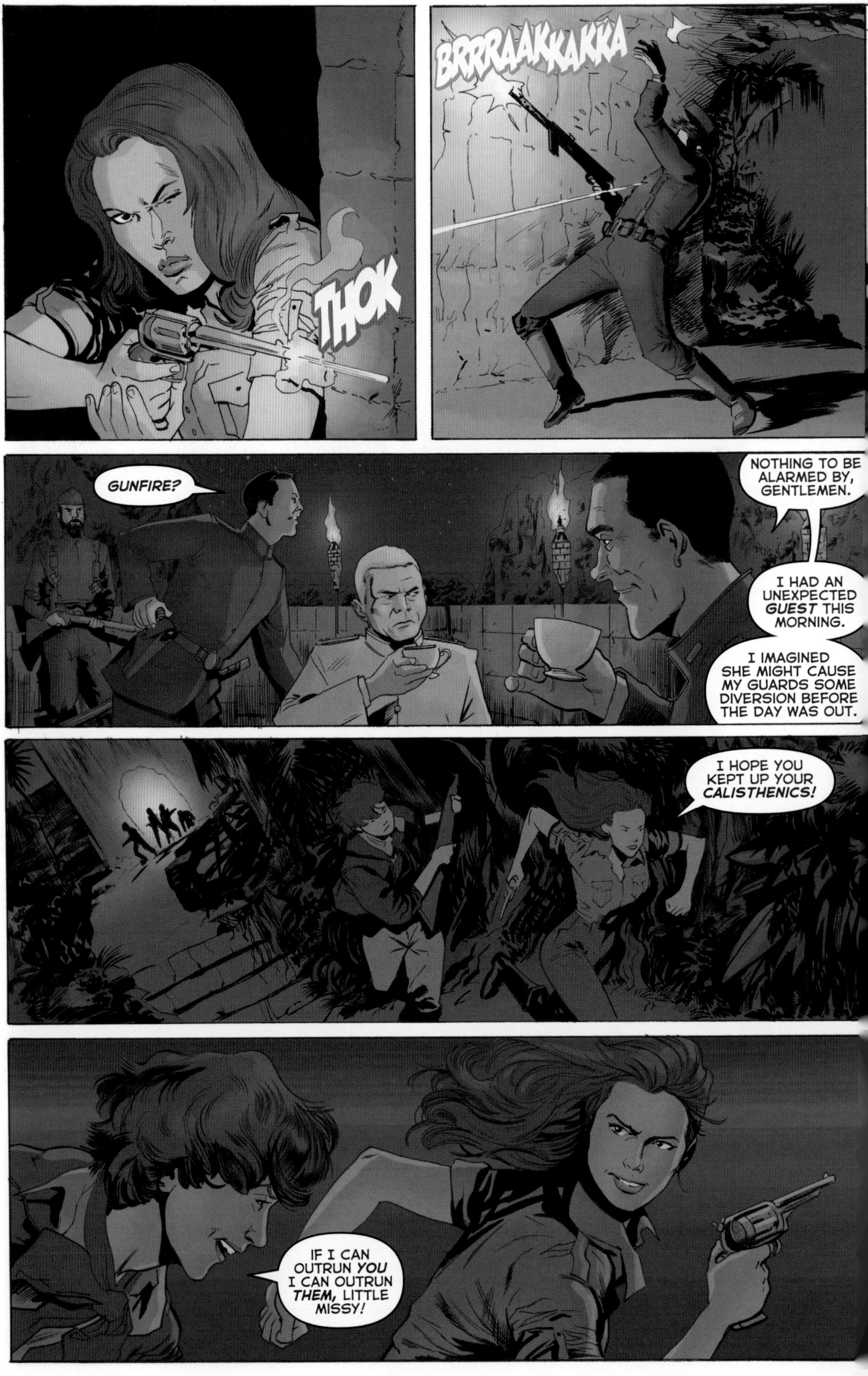
THOK
BRRRAAKKAKKA
GUNFIRE?
NOTHING TO BE ALARMED BY, GENTLEMEN.
I HAD AN UNEXPECTED GUEST THIS MORNING.
I IMAGINED SHE MIGHT CAUSE MY GUARDS SOME DIVERSION BEFORE THE DAY WAS OUT.
I HOPE YOU KEPT UP YOUR CALISTHENICS!
IF I CAN OUTRUN YOU I CAN OUTRUN THEM, LITTLE MISSY!

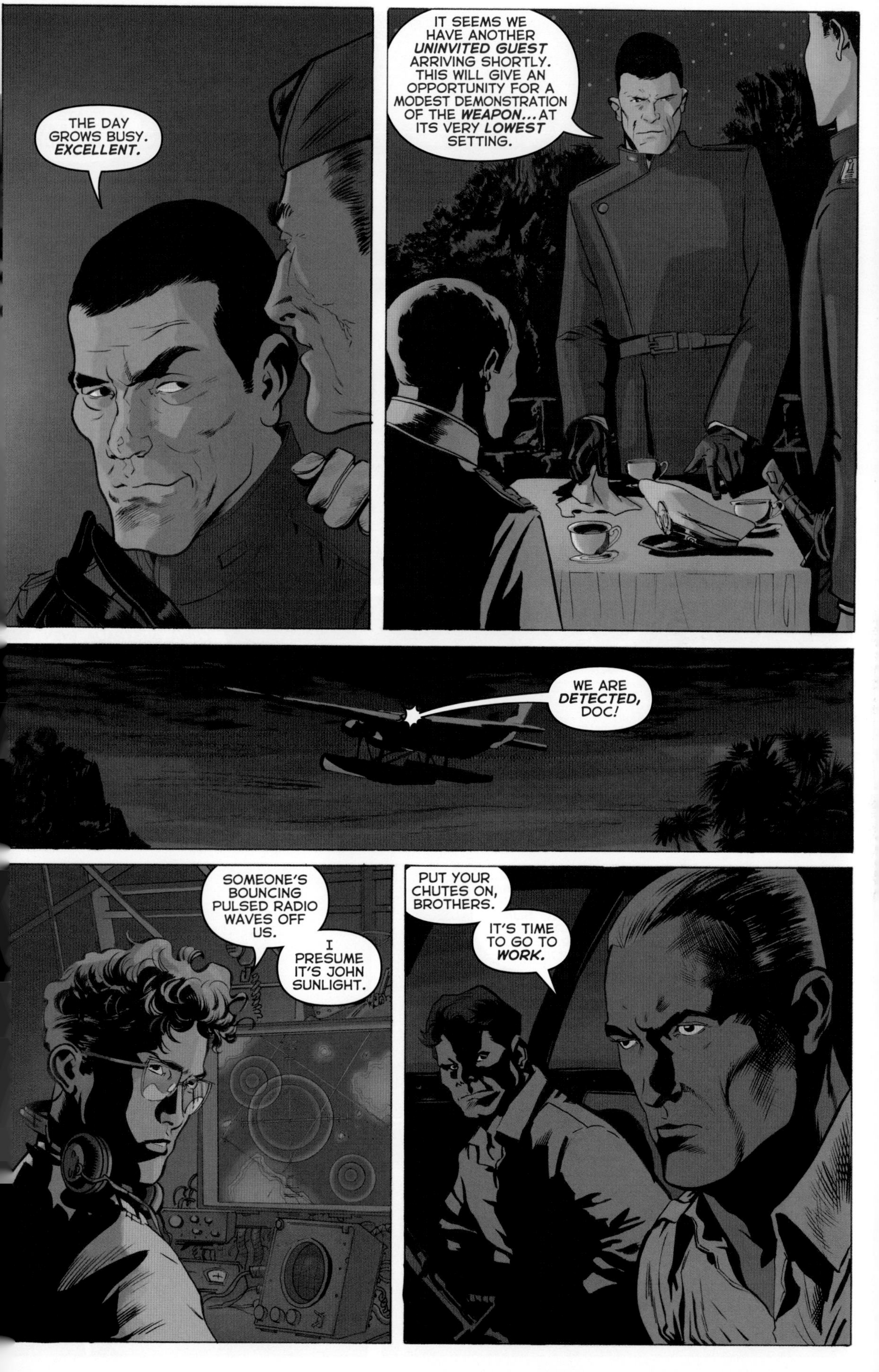
THE DAY GROWS BUSY. EXCELLENT.
IT SEEMS WE HAVE ANOTHER UNINVITED GUEST ARRIVING SHORTLY. THIS WILL GIVE AN OPPORTUNITY FOR A MODEST DEMONSTRATION OF THE WEAPON... AT ITS VERY LOWEST SETTING.
WE ARE DETECTED, DOC!
SOMEONE'S BOUNCING PULSED RADIO WAVES OFF US.
I PRESUME IT'S JOHN SUNLIGHT.
PUT YOUR CHUTES ON, BROTHERS.
IT'S TIME TO GO TO WORK.

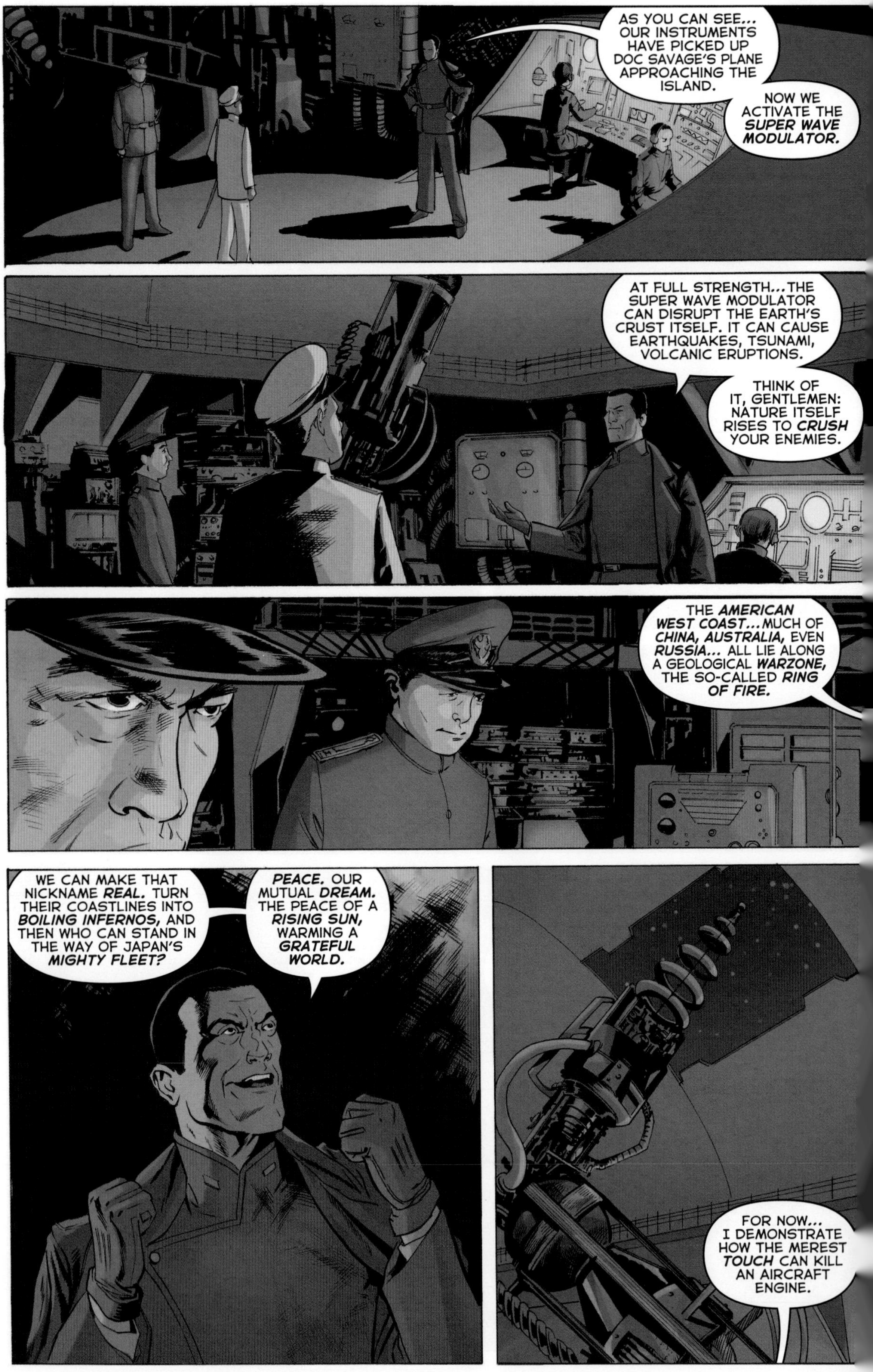
AS YOU CAN SEE... OUR INSTRUMENTS HAVE PICKED UP DOC SAVAGE'S PLANE APPROACHING THE ISLAND.
NOW WE ACTIVATE THE *SUPER WAVE MODULATOR.*
AT FULL STRENGTH... THE SUPER WAVE MODULATOR CAN DISRUPT THE EARTH'S CRUST ITSELF. IT CAN CAUSE EARTHQUAKES, TSUNAMI, VOLCANIC ERUPTIONS.
THINK OF IT, GENTLEMEN: NATURE ITSELF RISES TO *CRUSH* YOUR ENEMIES.
THE *AMERICAN WEST COAST*... MUCH OF *CHINA, AUSTRALIA,* EVEN *RUSSIA*... ALL LIE ALONG A GEOLOGICAL *WARZONE,* THE SO-CALLED *RING OF FIRE.*
WE CAN MAKE THAT NICKNAME *REAL.* TURN THEIR COASTLINES INTO *BOILING INFERNOS,* AND THEN WHO CAN STAND IN THE WAY OF JAPAN'S *MIGHTY FLEET?*
PEACE. OUR MUTUAL *DREAM.* THE PEACE OF A *RISING SUN,* WARMING A *GRATEFUL WORLD.*
FOR NOW... I DEMONSTRATE HOW THE MEREST *TOUCH* CAN KILL AN AIRCRAFT ENGINE.

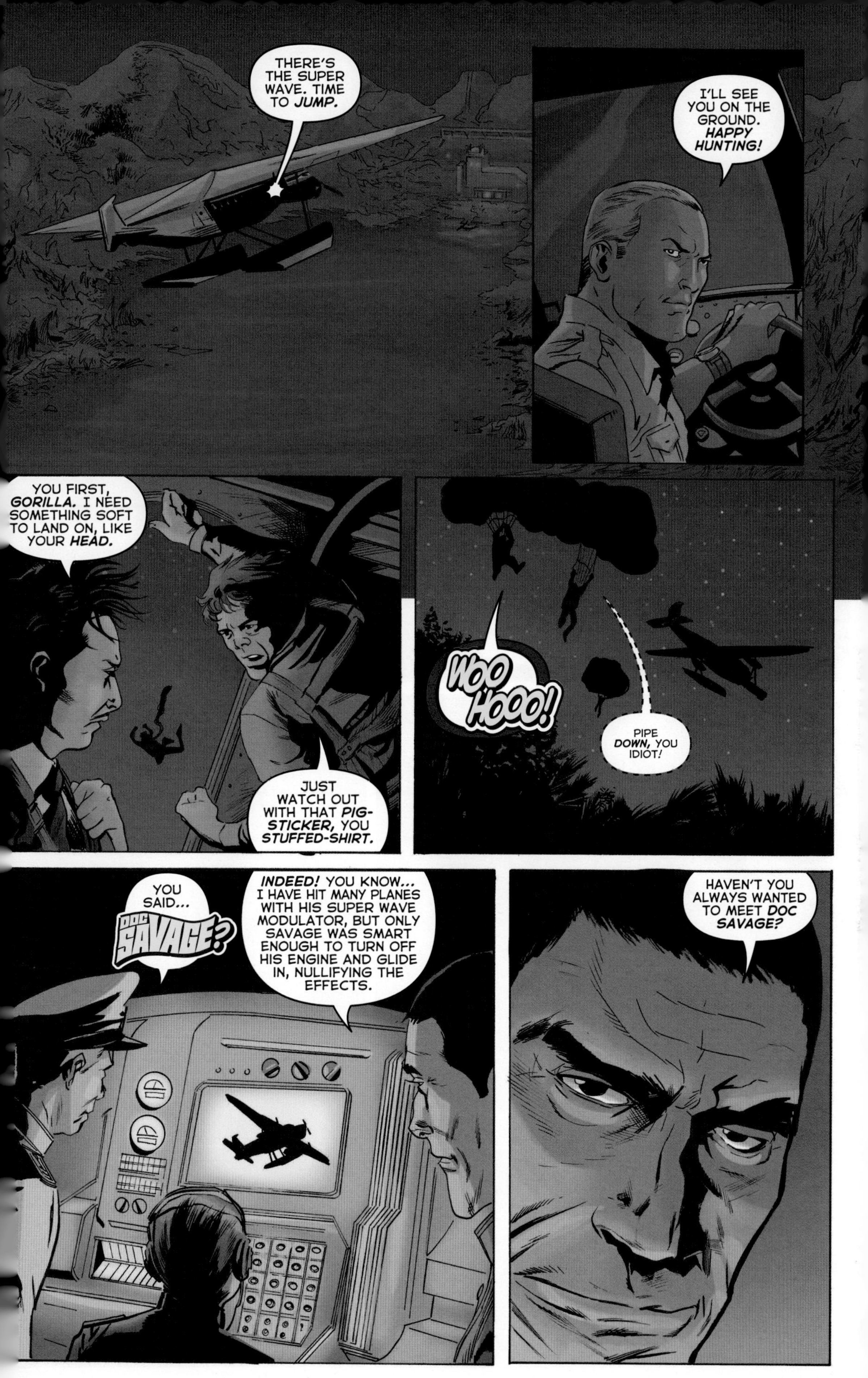
THERE'S THE SUPER WAVE. TIME TO JUMP.
I'LL SEE YOU ON THE GROUND. HAPPY HUNTING!
YOU FIRST, GORILLA. I NEED SOMETHING SOFT TO LAND ON, LIKE YOUR HEAD.
JUST WATCH OUT WITH THAT PIG-STICKER, YOU STUFFED-SHIRT.
WOO HOOO!
PIPE DOWN, YOU IDIOT!
YOU SAID... DOC SAVAGE?
INDEED! YOU KNOW... I HAVE HIT MANY PLANES WITH HIS SUPER WAVE MODULATOR, BUT ONLY SAVAGE WAS SMART ENOUGH TO TURN OFF HIS ENGINE AND GLIDE IN, NULLIFYING THE EFFECTS.
HAVEN'T YOU ALWAYS WANTED TO MEET DOC SAVAGE?

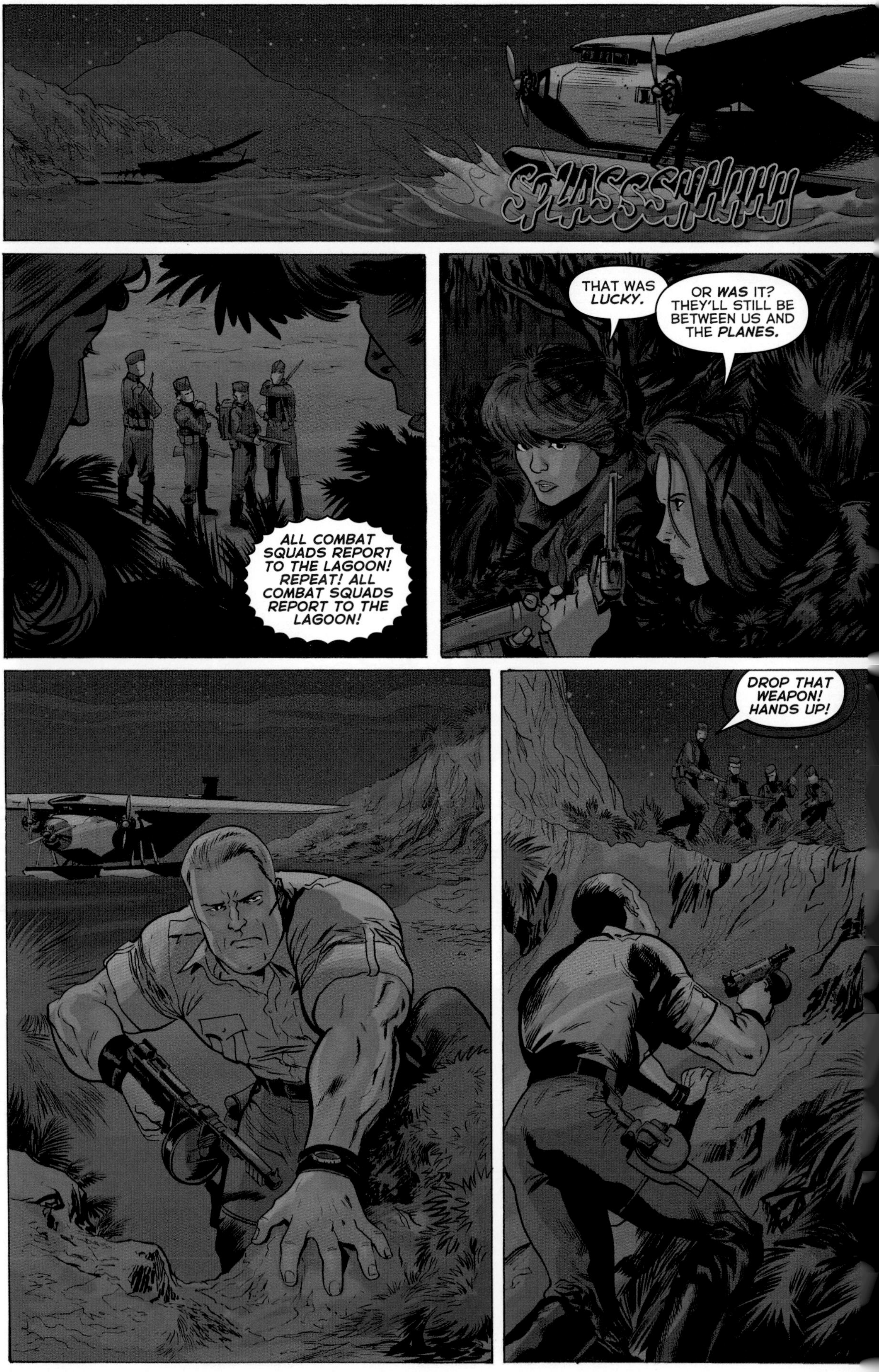
SPLASSSHHHH
ALL COMBAT SQUADS REPORT TO THE LAGOON! REPEAT! ALL COMBAT SQUADS REPORT TO THE LAGOON!
THAT WAS *LUCKY.*
OR *WAS* IT? THEY'LL STILL BE BETWEEN US AND THE *PLANES.*
DROP THAT WEAPON! HANDS UP!

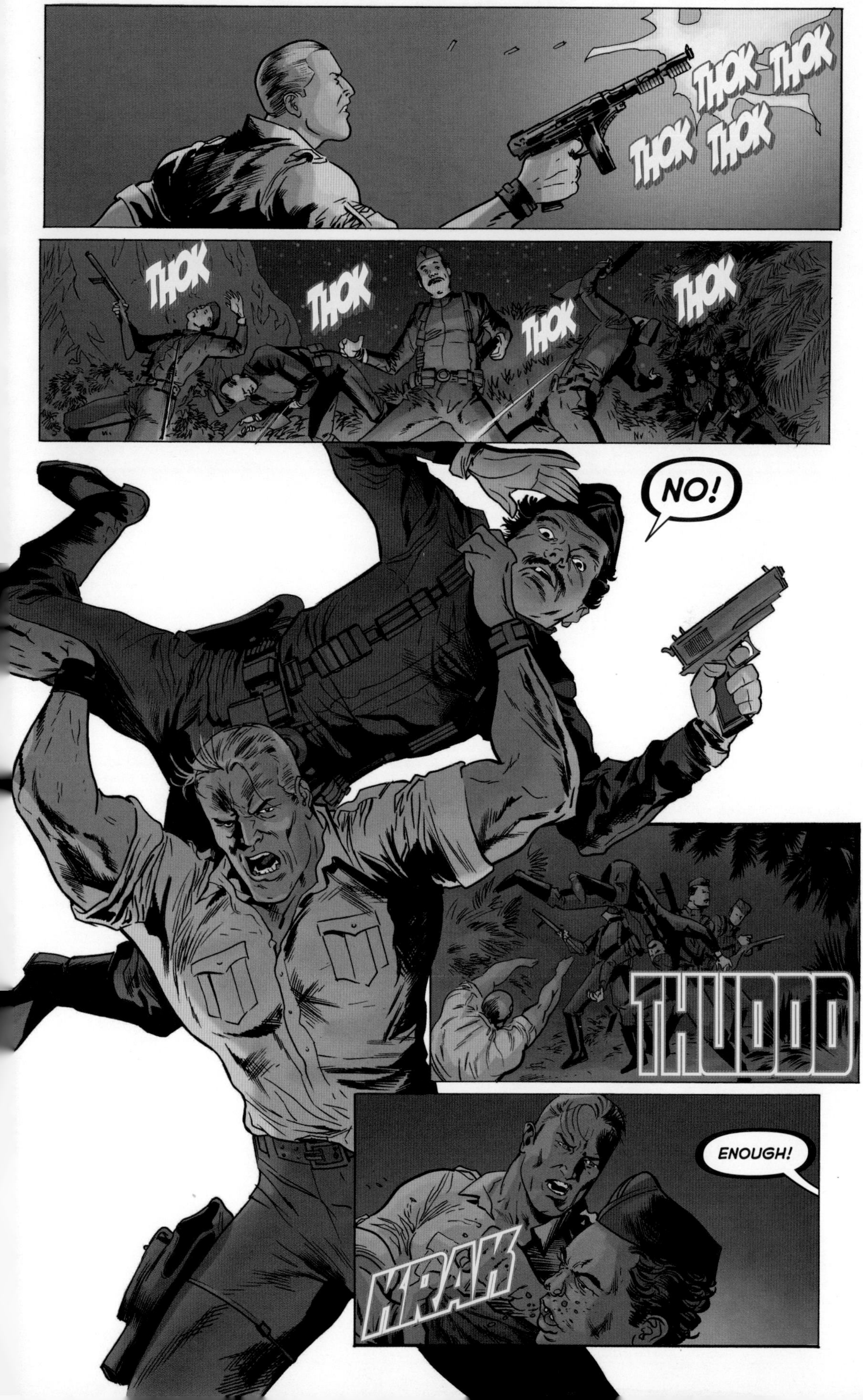
THOK THOK
THOK THOK
THOK
THOK
THOK
THOK
NO!
THUDDD
ENOUGH!
KRAK

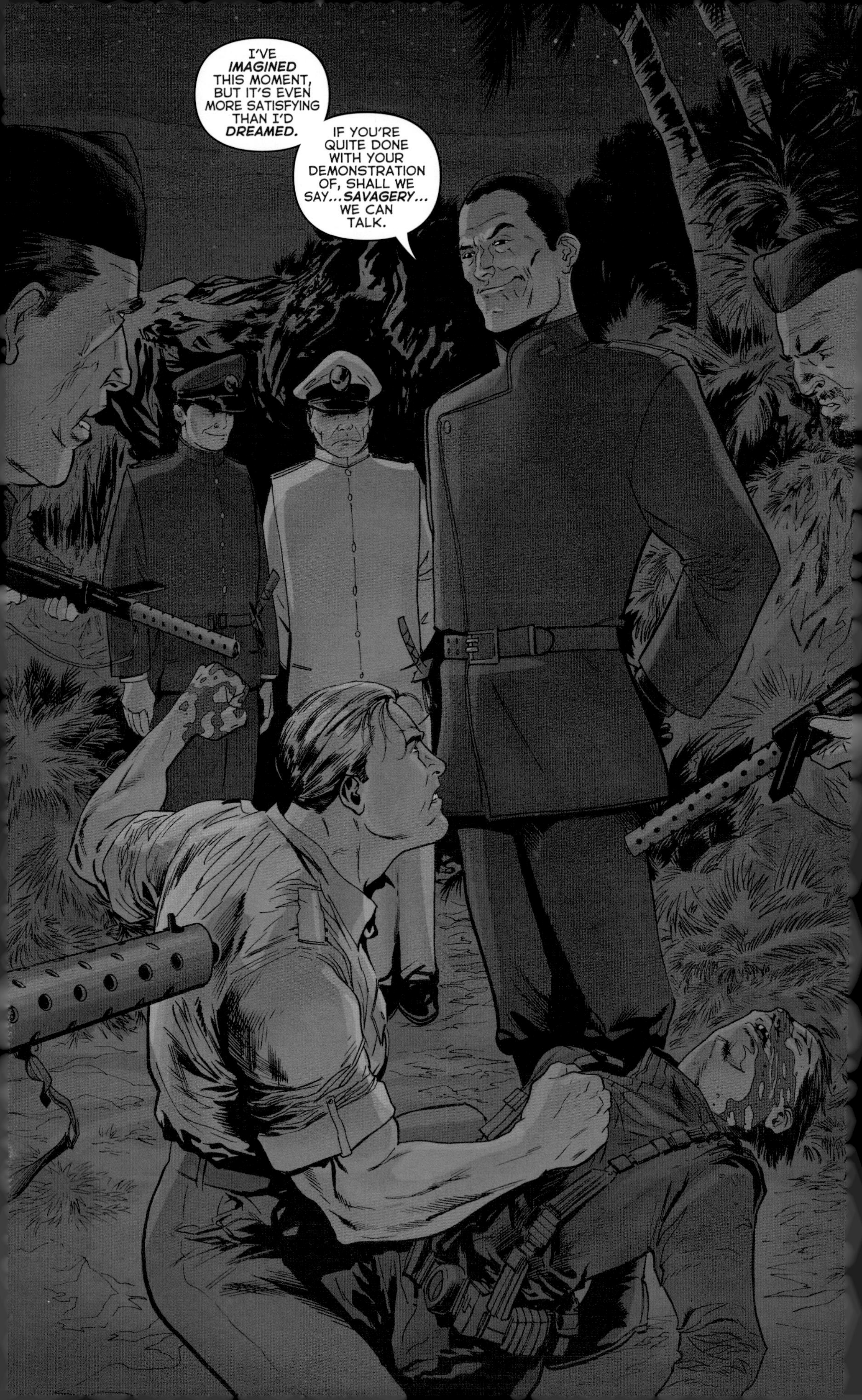
I'VE *IMAGINED* THIS MOMENT, BUT IT'S EVEN MORE SATISFYING THAN I'D *DREAMED.*
IF YOU'RE QUITE DONE WITH YOUR DEMONSTRATION OF, SHALL WE SAY...*SAVAGERY*... WE CAN TALK.

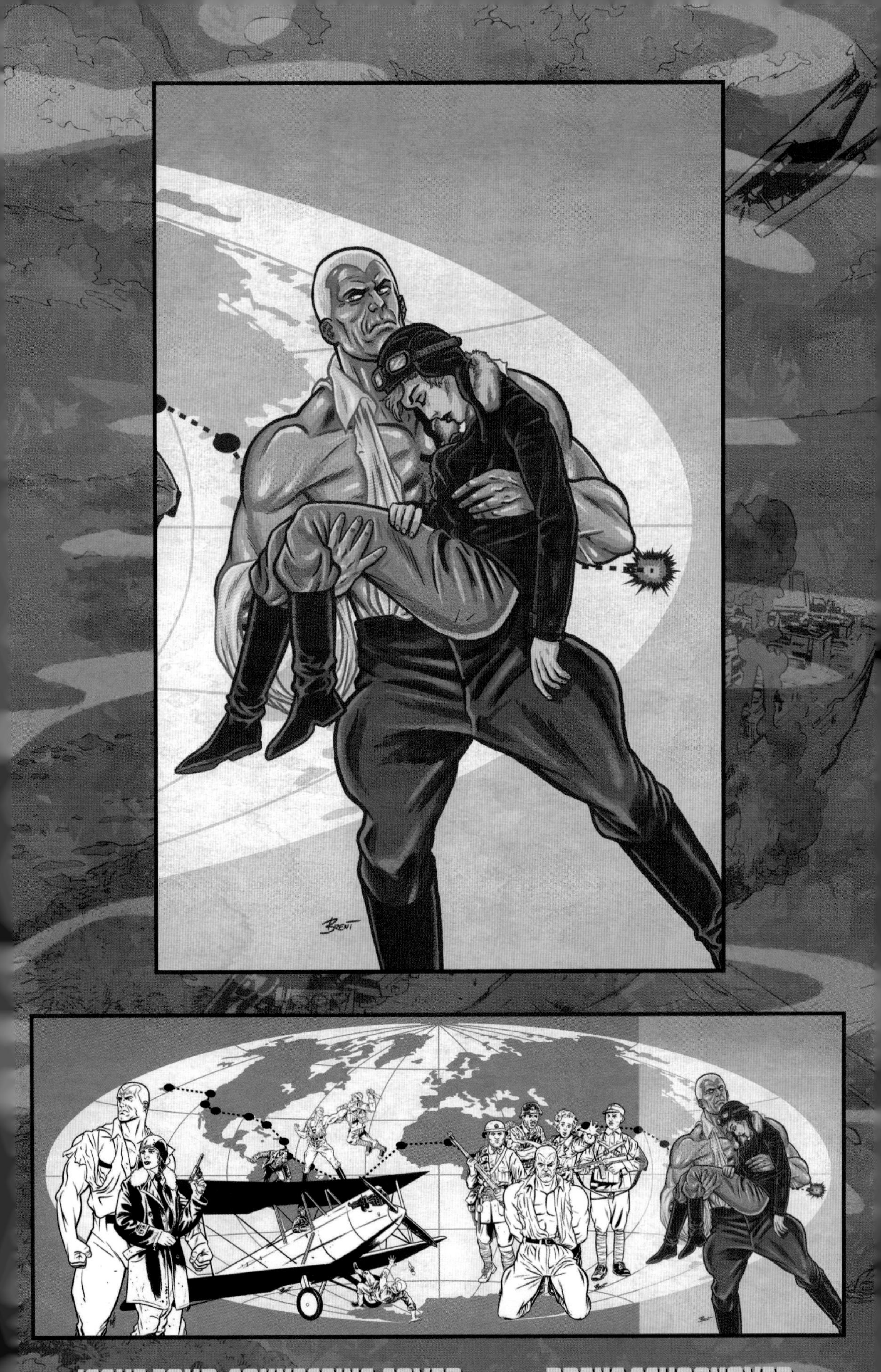
BRENT

ISSUE FOUR CONNECTING COVER ART BY BRENT SCHOONOVER

FOUR

"PHOENIX UNBOUND"

ISSUE FOUR VARIANT COVER art by **ANTHONY MARQUES**
inks by **J. BONE**, colors by **CHRIS O'HALLORAN**

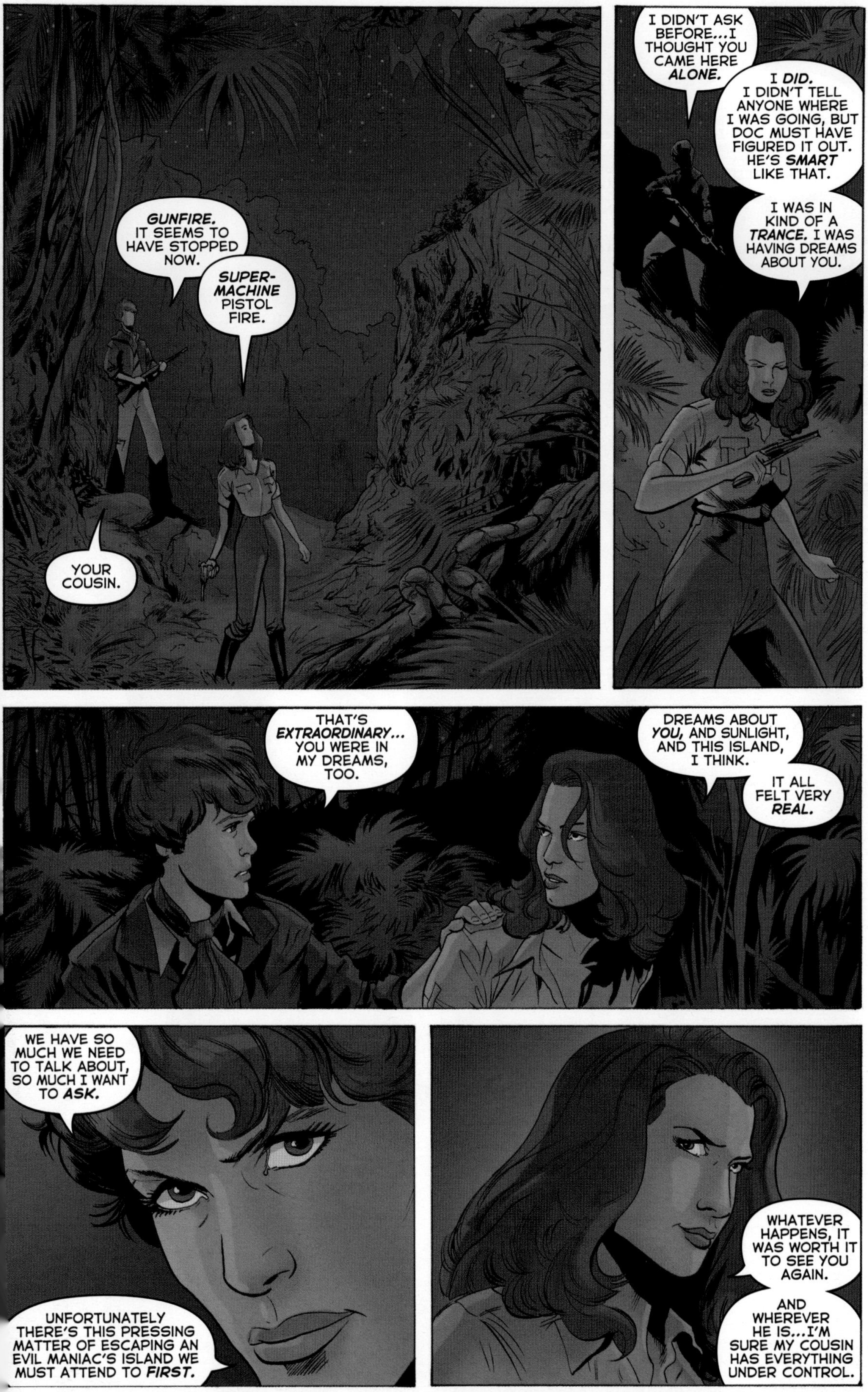
GUNFIRE. IT SEEMS TO HAVE STOPPED NOW.
SUPER-MACHINE PISTOL FIRE.
YOUR COUSIN.
I DIDN'T ASK BEFORE...I THOUGHT YOU CAME HERE ALONE.
I DID. I DIDN'T TELL ANYONE WHERE I WAS GOING, BUT DOC MUST HAVE FIGURED IT OUT. HE'S SMART LIKE THAT.
I WAS IN KIND OF A TRANCE. I WAS HAVING DREAMS ABOUT YOU.
THAT'S EXTRAORDINARY... YOU WERE IN MY DREAMS, TOO.
DREAMS ABOUT YOU, AND SUNLIGHT, AND THIS ISLAND, I THINK.
IT ALL FELT VERY REAL.
WE HAVE SO MUCH WE NEED TO TALK ABOUT, SO MUCH I WANT TO ASK.
UNFORTUNATELY THERE'S THIS PRESSING MATTER OF ESCAPING AN EVIL MANIAC'S ISLAND WE MUST ATTEND TO FIRST.
WHATEVER HAPPENS, IT WAS WORTH IT TO SEE YOU AGAIN.
AND WHEREVER HE IS...I'M SURE MY COUSIN HAS EVERYTHING UNDER CONTROL.

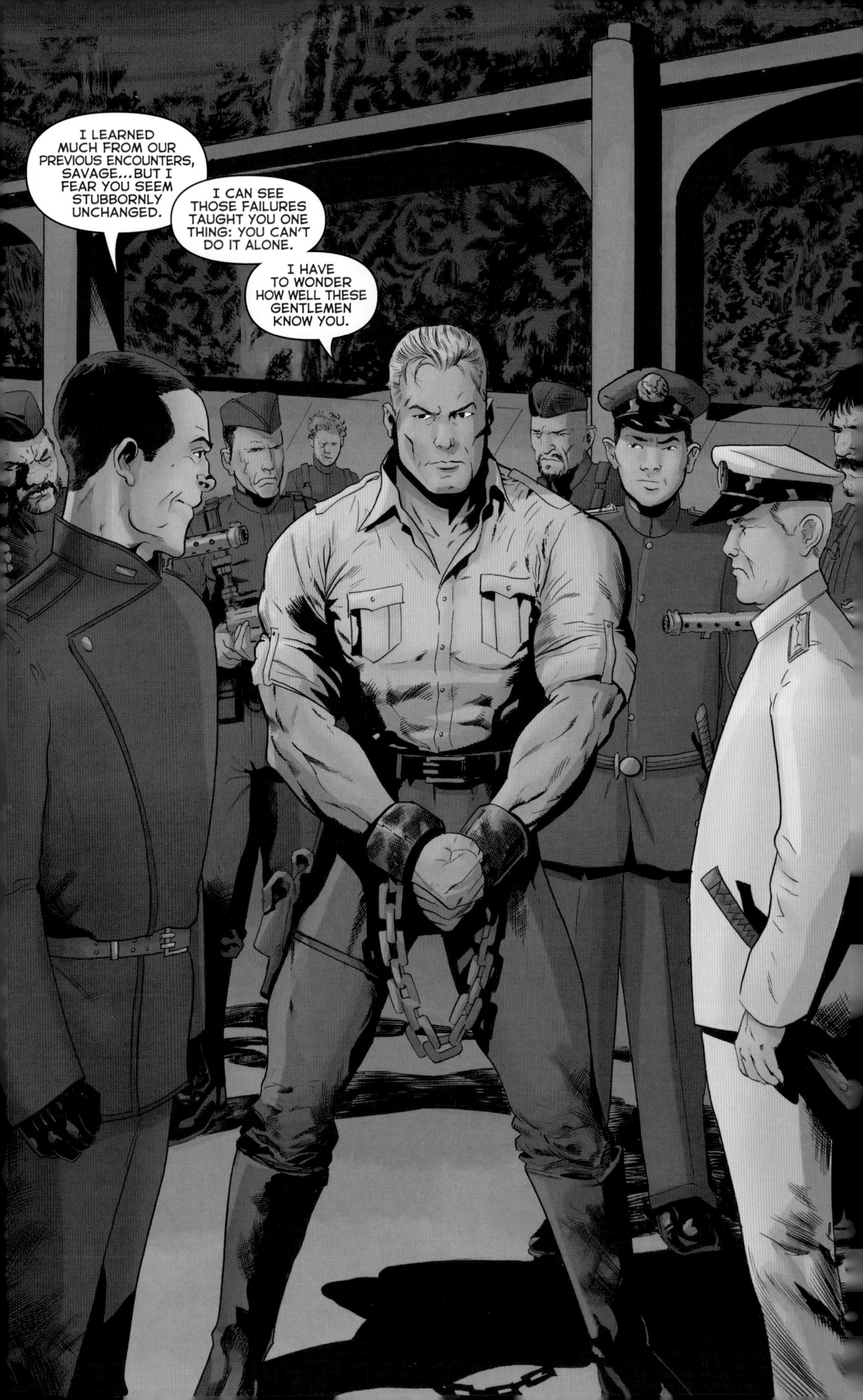
I LEARNED MUCH FROM OUR PREVIOUS ENCOUNTERS, SAVAGE...BUT I FEAR YOU SEEM STUBBORNLY UNCHANGED.
I CAN SEE THOSE FAILURES TAUGHT YOU ONE THING: YOU CAN'T DO IT ALONE.
I HAVE TO WONDER HOW WELL THESE GENTLEMEN KNOW YOU.

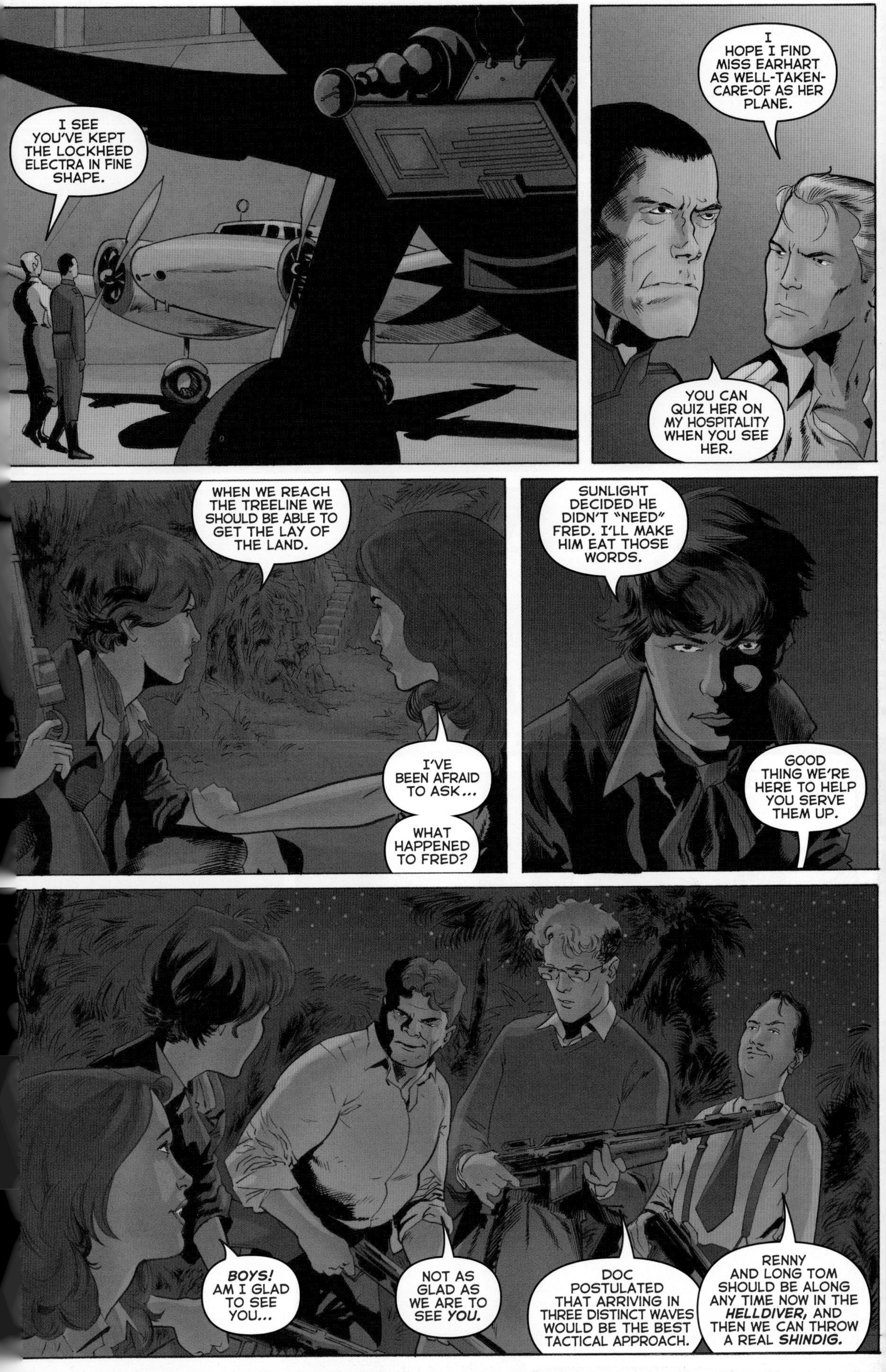

I SEE YOU'VE KEPT THE LOCKHEED ELECTRA IN FINE SHAPE.
I HOPE I FIND MISS EARHART AS WELL-TAKEN-CARE-OF AS HER PLANE.
YOU CAN QUIZ HER ON MY HOSPITALITY WHEN YOU SEE HER.
WHEN WE REACH THE TREELINE WE SHOULD BE ABLE TO GET THE LAY OF THE LAND.
I'VE BEEN AFRAID TO ASK...
WHAT HAPPENED TO FRED?
SUNLIGHT DECIDED HE DIDN'T "NEED" FRED. I'LL MAKE HIM EAT THOSE WORDS.
GOOD THING WE'RE HERE TO HELP YOU SERVE THEM UP.
BOYS! AM I GLAD TO SEE YOU...
NOT AS GLAD AS WE ARE TO SEE *YOU.*
DOC POSTULATED THAT ARRIVING IN THREE DISTINCT WAVES WOULD BE THE BEST TACTICAL APPROACH.
RENNY AND LONG TOM SHOULD BE ALONG ANY TIME NOW IN THE *HELLDIVER,* AND THEN WE CAN THROW A REAL *SHINDIG.*

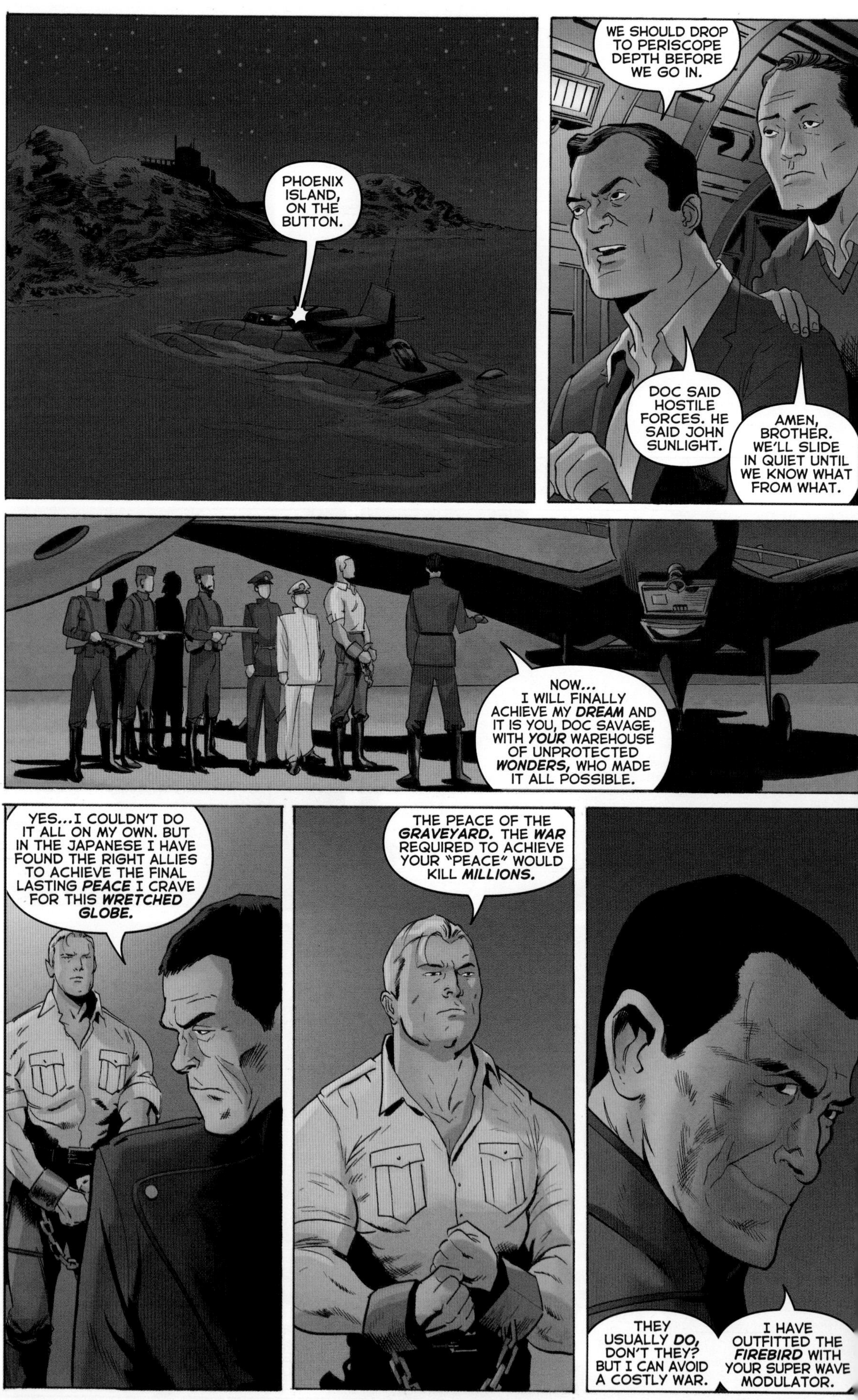
PHOENIX ISLAND, ON THE BUTTON.
WE SHOULD DROP TO PERISCOPE DEPTH BEFORE WE GO IN.
DOC SAID HOSTILE FORCES. HE SAID JOHN SUNLIGHT.
AMEN, BROTHER. WE'LL SLIDE IN QUIET UNTIL WE KNOW WHAT FROM WHAT.
NOW... I WILL FINALLY ACHIEVE MY DREAM AND IT IS YOU, DOC SAVAGE, WITH YOUR WAREHOUSE OF UNPROTECTED WONDERS, WHO MADE IT ALL POSSIBLE.
YES...I COULDN'T DO IT ALL ON MY OWN. BUT IN THE JAPANESE I HAVE FOUND THE RIGHT ALLIES TO ACHIEVE THE FINAL LASTING PEACE I CRAVE FOR THIS WRETCHED GLOBE.
THE PEACE OF THE GRAVEYARD. THE WAR REQUIRED TO ACHIEVE YOUR "PEACE" WOULD KILL MILLIONS.
THEY USUALLY DO, DON'T THEY? BUT I CAN AVOID A COSTLY WAR.
I HAVE OUTFITTED THE FIREBIRD WITH YOUR SUPER WAVE MODULATOR.

IT STANDS READY: IT WILL FLY TO SAN FRANCISCO, AND *DESTROY* THE *ENTIRE CITY* WITH THE FLICK OF A DIAL.

AND I WILL TELL THE WORLD HOW IT WAS *DONE.*

I WILL TELL THEM THAT *DOC SAVAGE* GAVE ME THE WEAPON, AND THAT LOS ANGELES IS *NEXT.*

AMERICA WILL CAPITULATE IN SHEER *TERROR.*

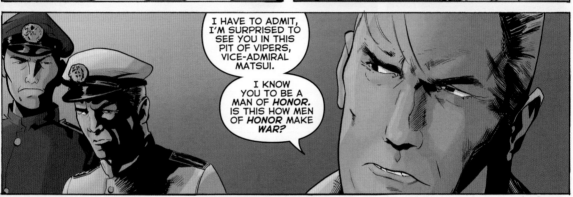

I HAVE TO ADMIT, I'M SURPRISED TO SEE YOU IN THIS PIT OF VIPERS, VICE-ADMIRAL MATSUI.

I KNOW YOU TO BE A MAN OF *HONOR.* IS THIS HOW MEN OF *HONOR* MAKE *WAR?*

THIS...MACHINE IS AN *ABOMINATION* IT IS A *COWARD'S* WEAPON, KILLING INNOCENTS FROM DISTANCE, RISKING *NOTHING.*

THERE IS NO *HONOR,* NO *COURAGE,* NO *HONESTY,* NO *MORALITY* IN SUCH A THING.

I WILL COUNSEL THE EMPEROR TO REJECT THIS *MADNESS.*

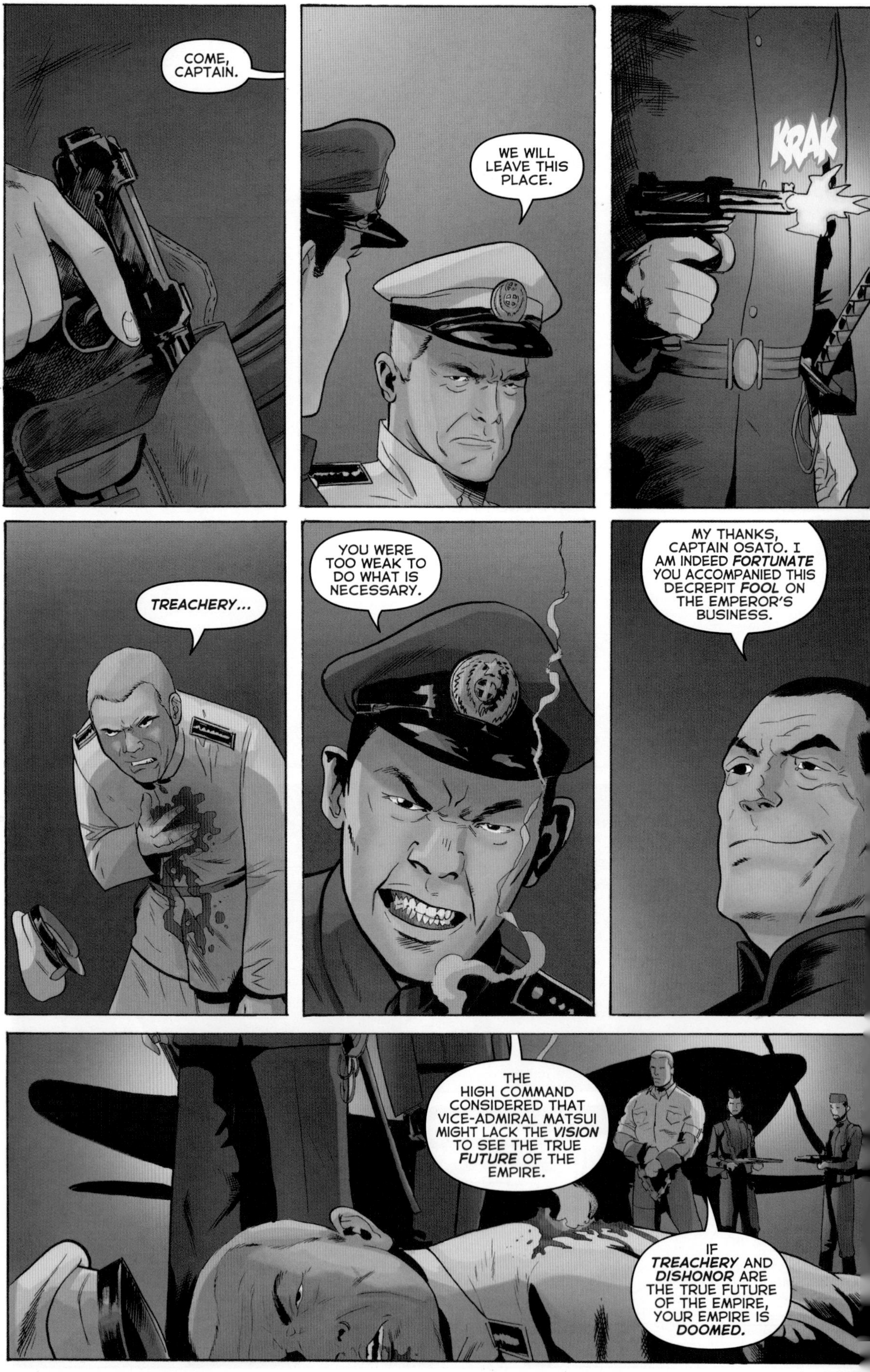
COME, CAPTAIN.
WE WILL LEAVE THIS PLACE.
KRAK
TREACHERY...
YOU WERE TOO WEAK TO DO WHAT IS NECESSARY.
MY THANKS, CAPTAIN OSATO. I AM INDEED FORTUNATE YOU ACCOMPANIED THIS DECREPIT FOOL ON THE EMPEROR'S BUSINESS.
THE HIGH COMMAND CONSIDERED THAT VICE-ADMIRAL MATSUI MIGHT LACK THE VISION TO SEE THE TRUE FUTURE OF THE EMPIRE.
IF TREACHERY AND DISHONOR ARE THE TRUE FUTURE OF THE EMPIRE, YOUR EMPIRE IS DOOMED.

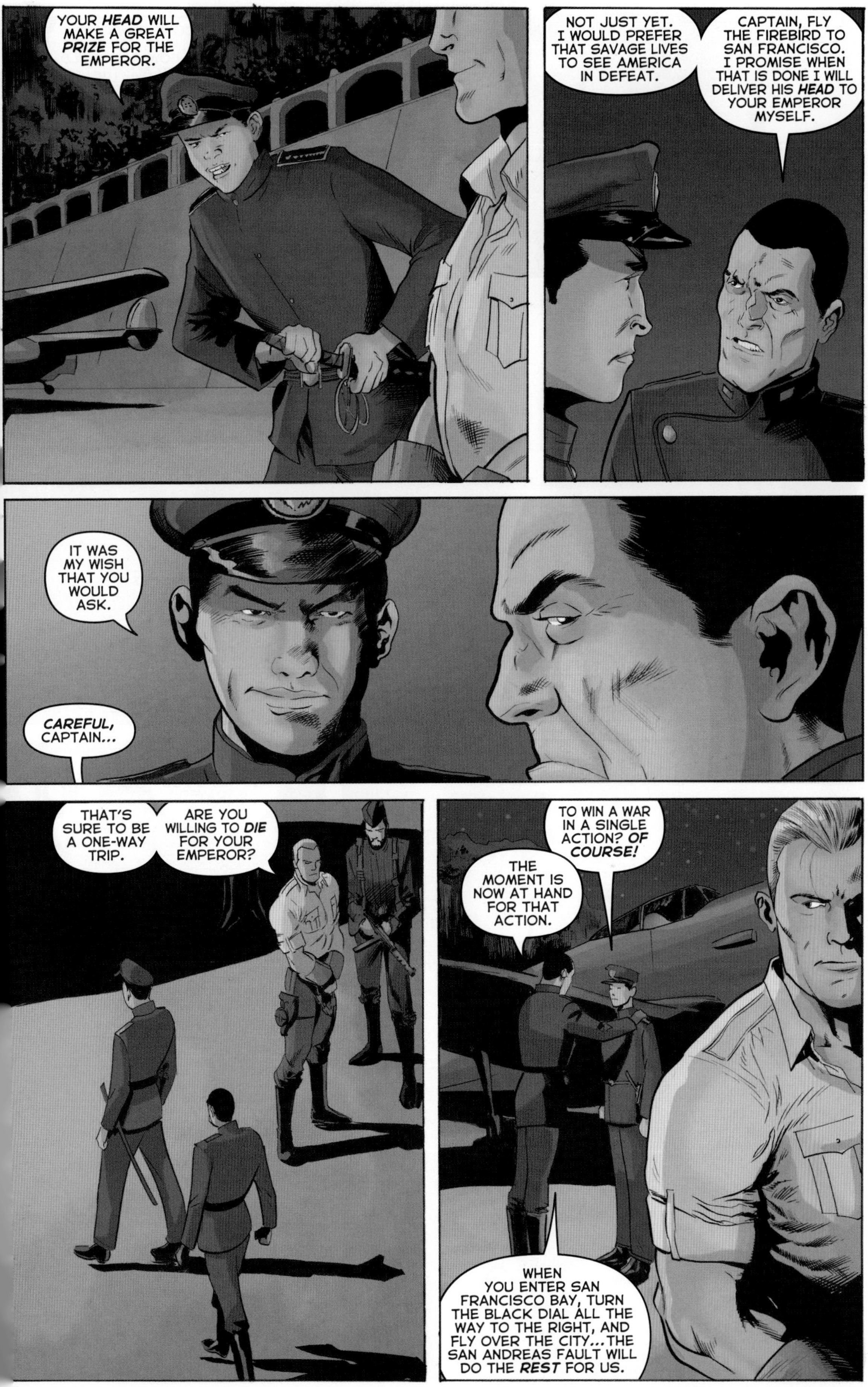
YOUR HEAD WILL MAKE A GREAT PRIZE FOR THE EMPEROR.
NOT JUST YET. I WOULD PREFER THAT SAVAGE LIVES TO SEE AMERICA IN DEFEAT.
CAPTAIN, FLY THE FIREBIRD TO SAN FRANCISCO. I PROMISE WHEN THAT IS DONE I WILL DELIVER HIS HEAD TO YOUR EMPEROR MYSELF.
IT WAS MY WISH THAT YOU WOULD ASK.
CAREFUL, CAPTAIN...
THAT'S SURE TO BE A ONE-WAY TRIP.
ARE YOU WILLING TO DIE FOR YOUR EMPEROR?
TO WIN A WAR IN A SINGLE ACTION? OF COURSE!
THE MOMENT IS NOW AT HAND FOR THAT ACTION.
WHEN YOU ENTER SAN FRANCISCO BAY, TURN THE BLACK DIAL ALL THE WAY TO THE RIGHT, AND FLY OVER THE CITY... THE SAN ANDREAS FAULT WILL DO THE REST FOR US.

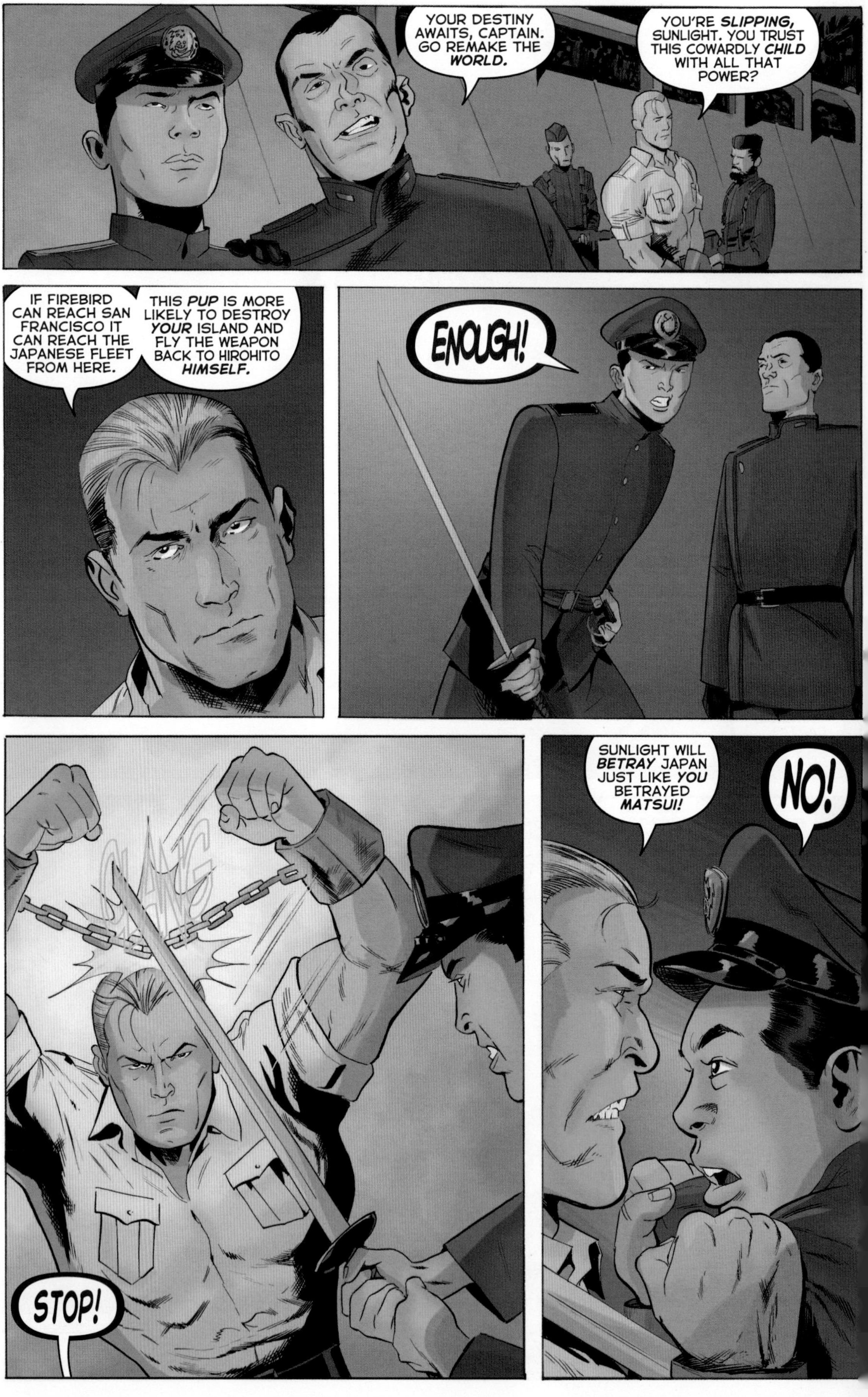
YOUR DESTINY AWAITS, CAPTAIN. GO REMAKE THE WORLD.
YOU'RE SLIPPING, SUNLIGHT. YOU TRUST THIS COWARDLY CHILD WITH ALL THAT POWER?
IF FIREBIRD CAN REACH SAN FRANCISCO IT CAN REACH THE JAPANESE FLEET FROM HERE.
THIS PUP IS MORE LIKELY TO DESTROY YOUR ISLAND AND FLY THE WEAPON BACK TO HIROHITO HIMSELF.
ENOUGH!
CLANG
STOP!
SUNLIGHT WILL BETRAY JAPAN JUST LIKE YOU BETRAYED MATSUI!
NO!

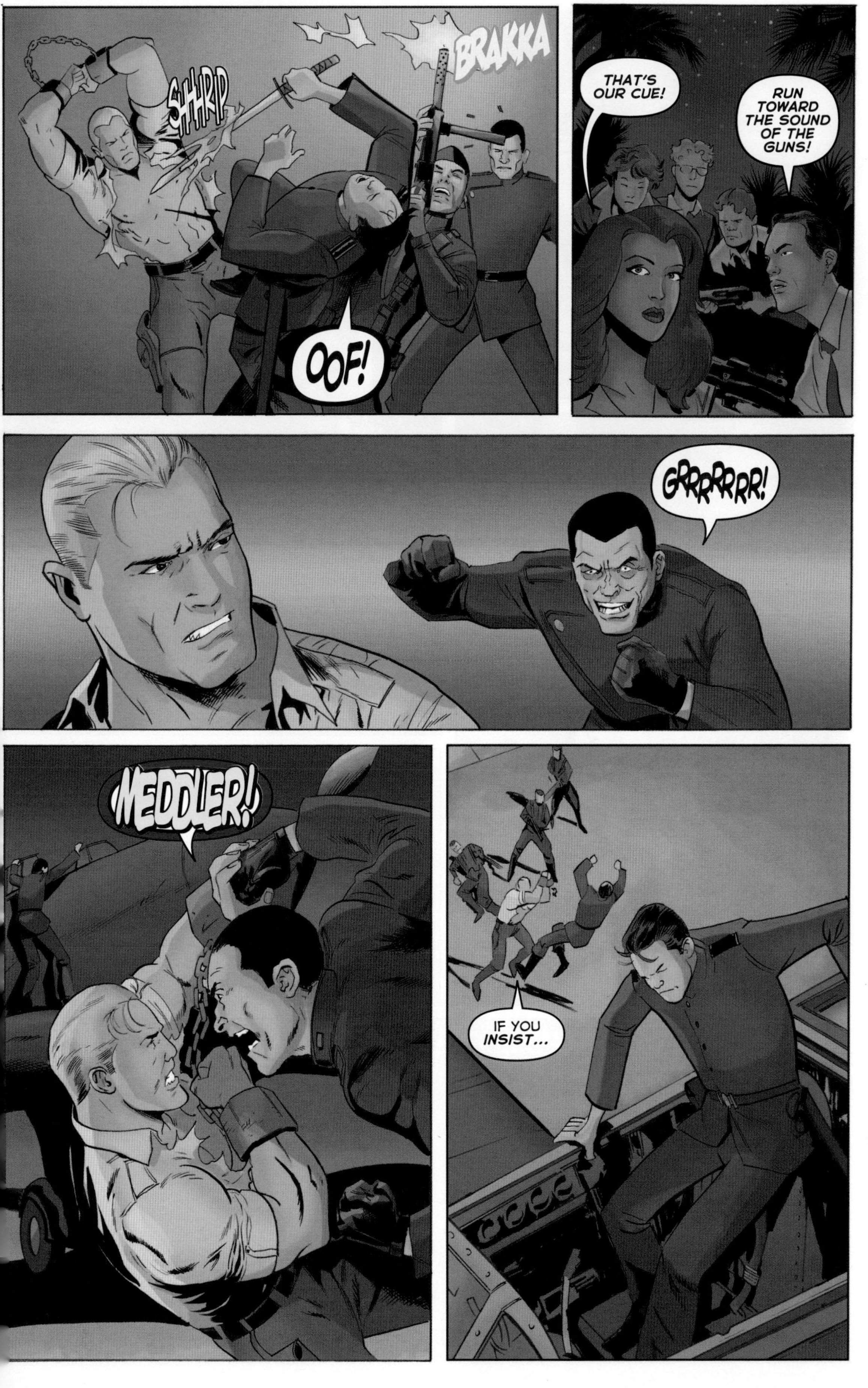
SHHRIP
BRAKKA
OOF!
THAT'S OUR CUE!
RUN TOWARD THE SOUND OF THE GUNS!
GRRRRRRR!
MEDDLER!
IF YOU INSIST...

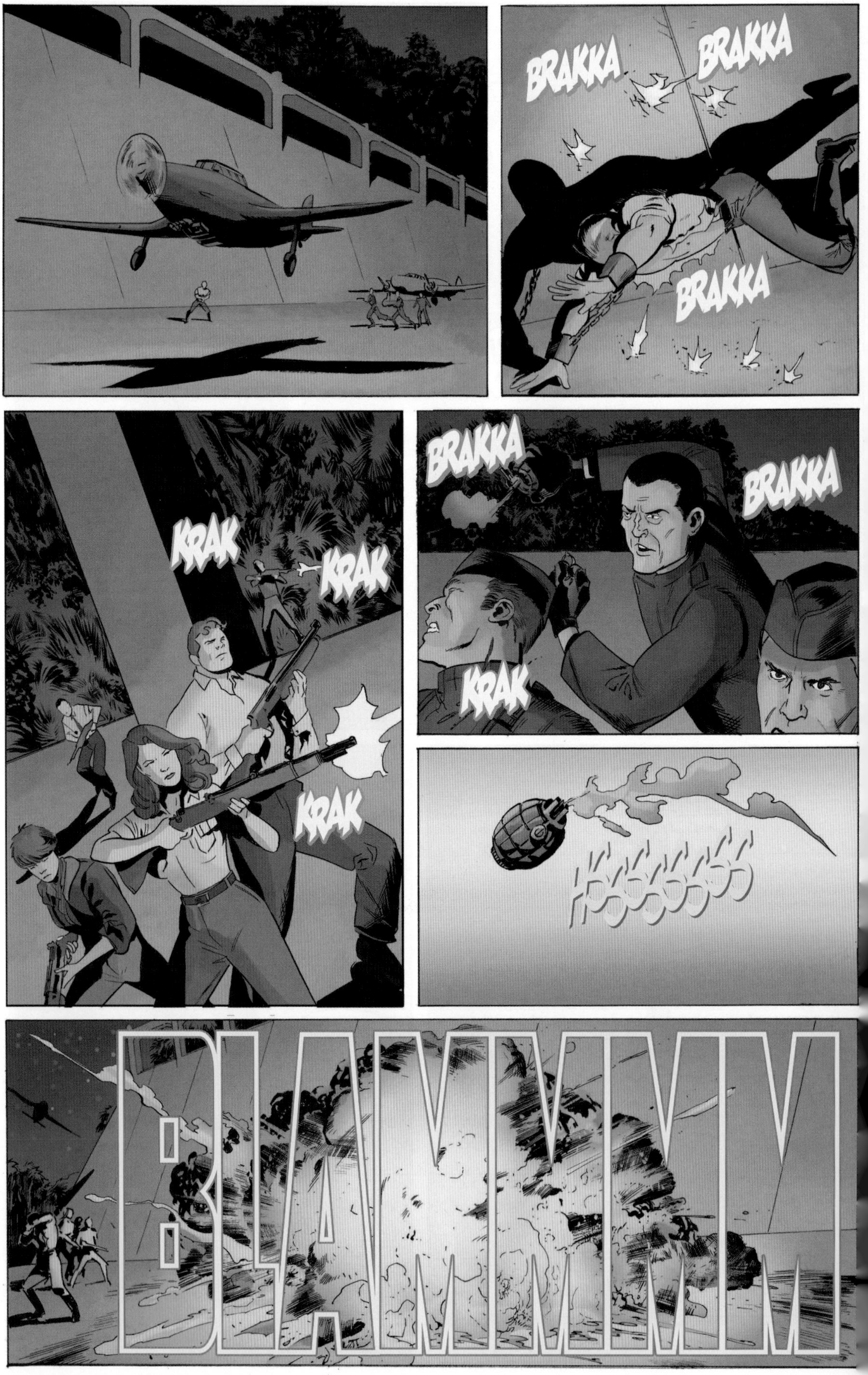
BRAKKA
BRAKKA
BRAKKA
KRAK
KRAK
KRAK
BRAKKA
BRAKKA
KRAK
HSSSSSSSS
BLAMMMM

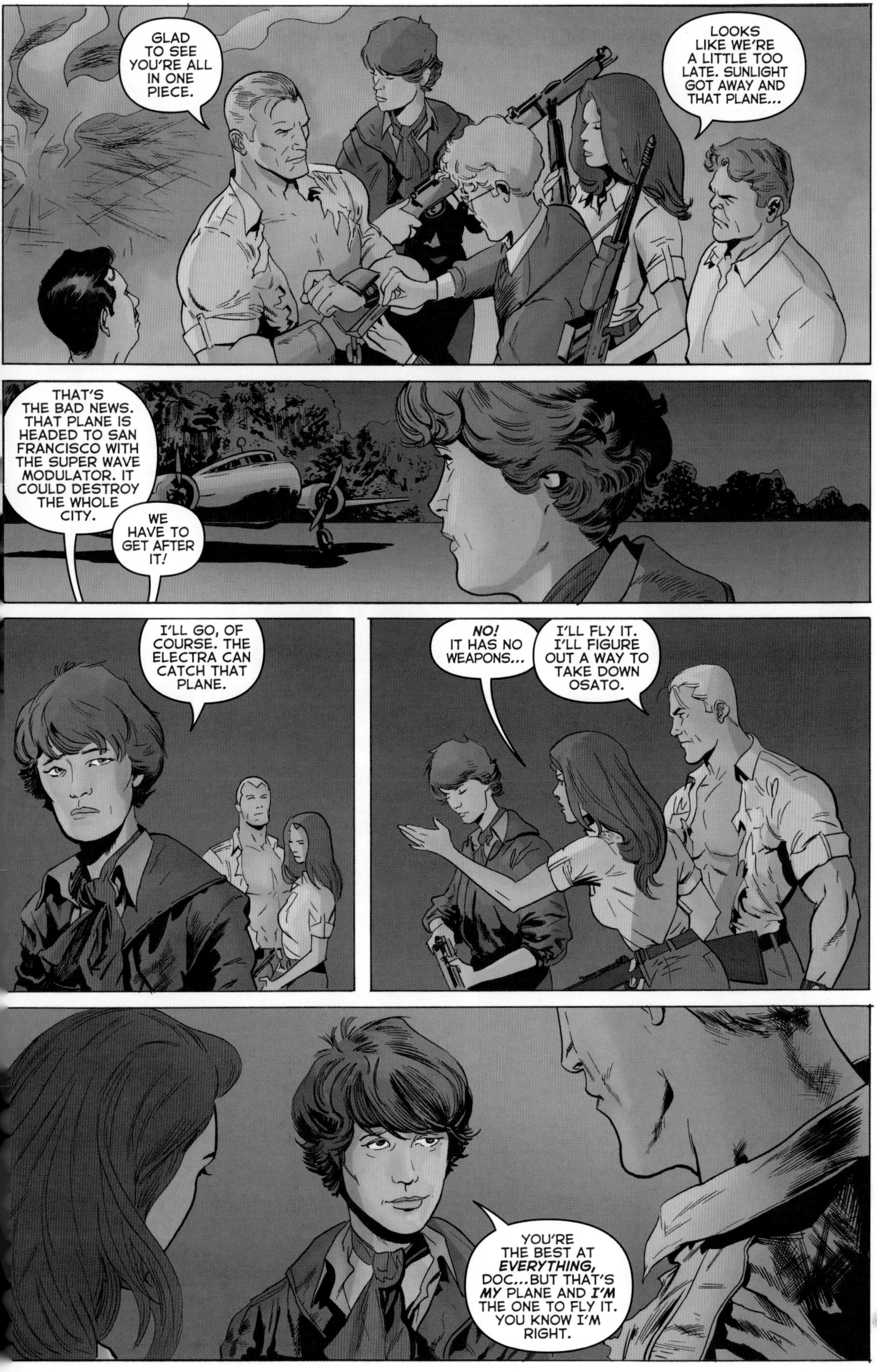
GLAD TO SEE YOU'RE ALL IN ONE PIECE.
LOOKS LIKE WE'RE A LITTLE TOO LATE. SUNLIGHT GOT AWAY AND THAT PLANE...
THAT'S THE BAD NEWS. THAT PLANE IS HEADED TO SAN FRANCISCO WITH THE SUPER WAVE MODULATOR. IT COULD DESTROY THE WHOLE CITY.
WE HAVE TO GET AFTER IT!
I'LL GO, OF COURSE. THE ELECTRA CAN CATCH THAT PLANE.
NO! IT HAS NO WEAPONS...
I'LL FLY IT. I'LL FIGURE OUT A WAY TO TAKE DOWN OSATO.
YOU'RE THE BEST AT ***EVERYTHING,*** DOC...BUT THAT'S ***MY*** PLANE AND ***I'M*** THE ONE TO FLY IT. YOU KNOW I'M RIGHT.

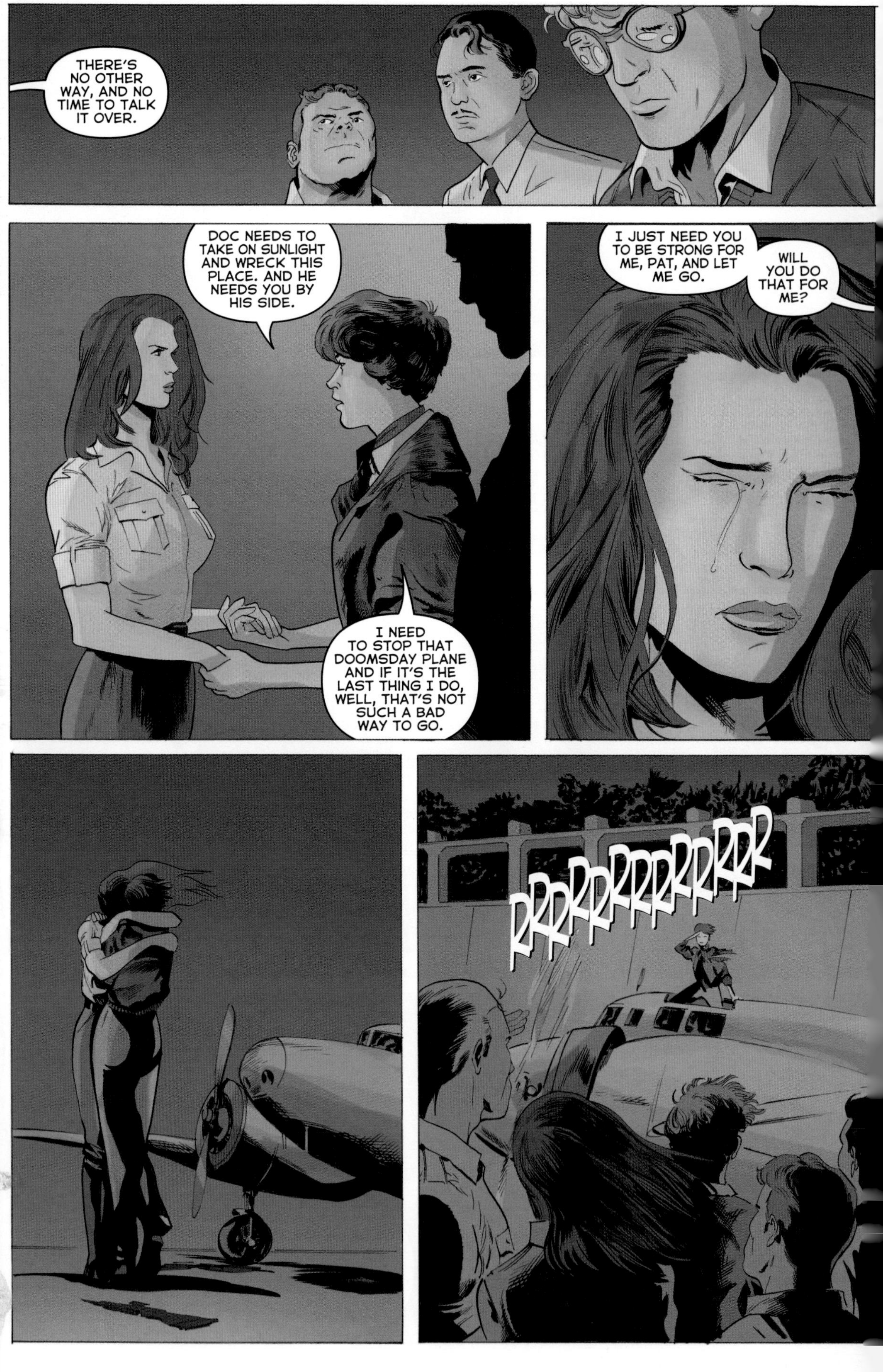

THERE'S NO OTHER WAY, AND NO TIME TO TALK IT OVER.
DOC NEEDS TO TAKE ON SUNLIGHT AND WRECK THIS PLACE. AND HE NEEDS YOU BY HIS SIDE.
I NEED TO STOP THAT DOOMSDAY PLANE AND IF IT'S THE LAST THING I DO, WELL, THAT'S NOT SUCH A BAD WAY TO GO.
I JUST NEED YOU TO BE STRONG FOR ME, PAT, AND LET ME GO.
WILL YOU DO THAT FOR ME?
RRRRRRRRRRRRRRR

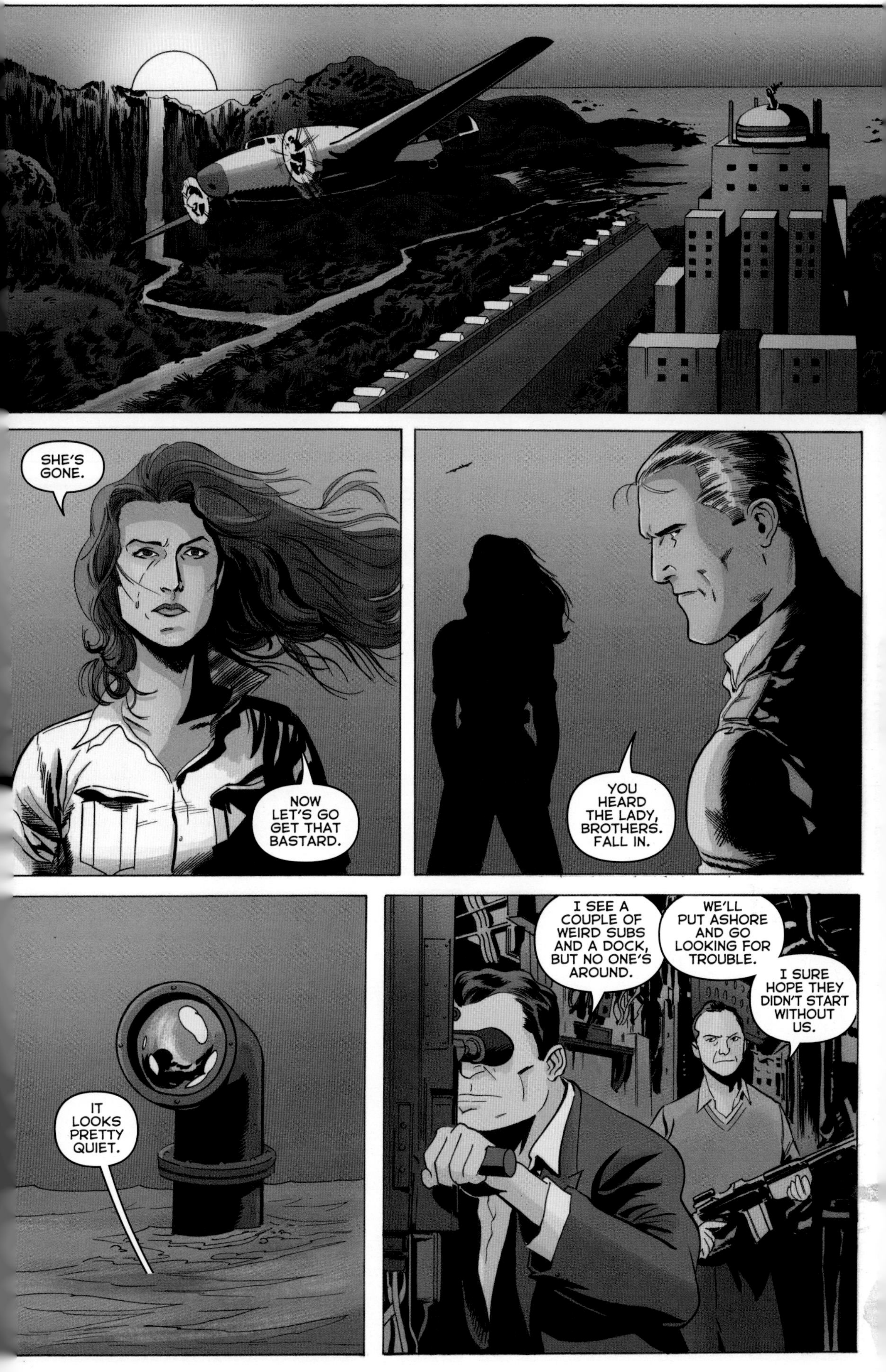
SHE'S GONE.
NOW LET'S GO GET THAT BASTARD.
YOU HEARD THE LADY, BROTHERS. FALL IN.
IT LOOKS PRETTY QUIET.
I SEE A COUPLE OF WEIRD SUBS AND A DOCK, BUT NO ONE'S AROUND.
WE'LL PUT ASHORE AND GO LOOKING FOR TROUBLE.
I SURE HOPE THEY DIDN'T START WITHOUT US.

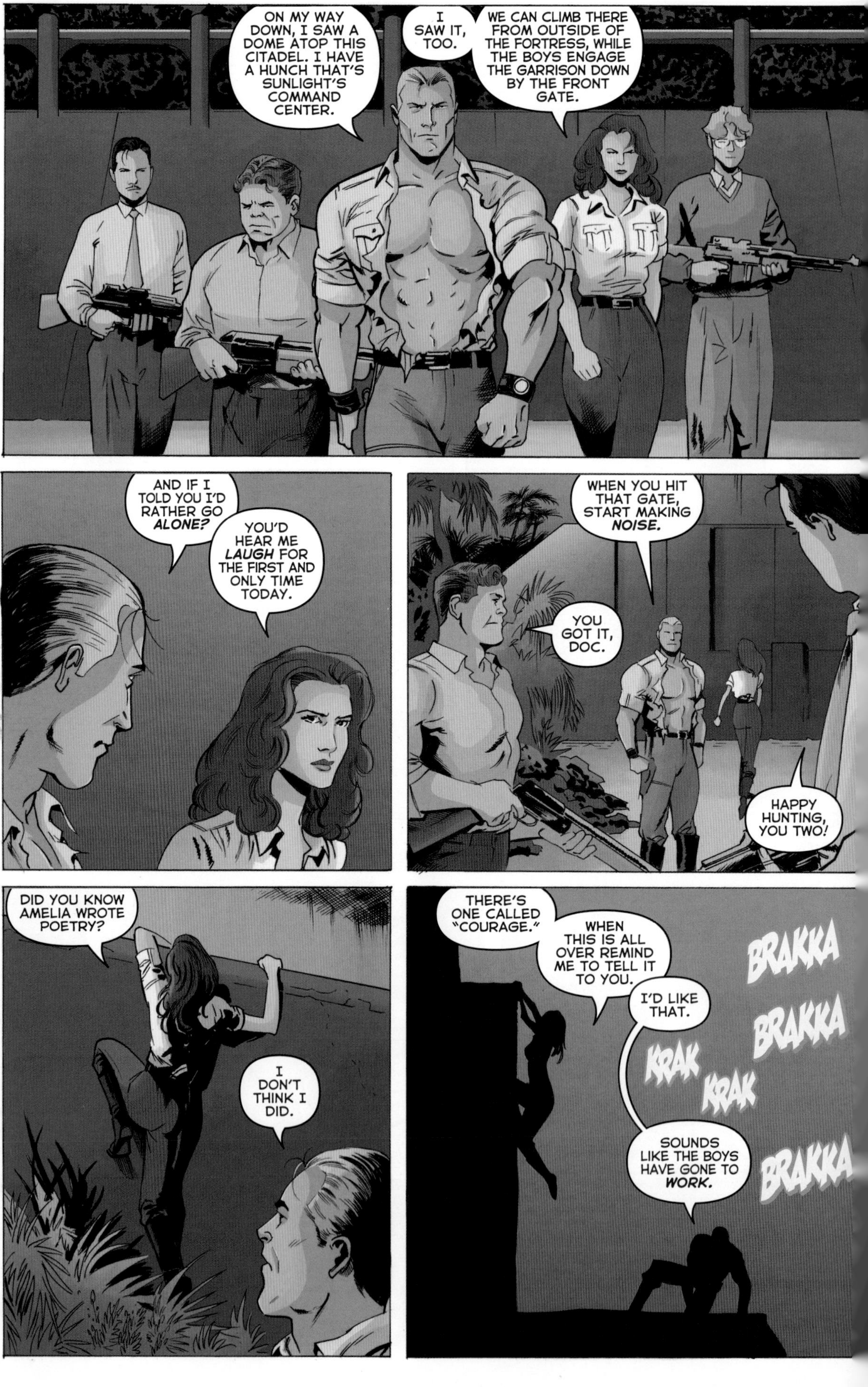

ON MY WAY DOWN, I SAW A DOME ATOP THIS CITADEL. I HAVE A HUNCH THAT'S SUNLIGHT'S COMMAND CENTER.
I SAW IT, TOO.
WE CAN CLIMB THERE FROM OUTSIDE OF THE FORTRESS, WHILE THE BOYS ENGAGE THE GARRISON DOWN BY THE FRONT GATE.
AND IF I TOLD YOU I'D RATHER GO *ALONE?*
YOU'D HEAR ME *LAUGH* FOR THE FIRST AND ONLY TIME TODAY.
WHEN YOU HIT THAT GATE, START MAKING *NOISE.*
YOU GOT IT, DOC.
HAPPY HUNTING, YOU TWO!
DID YOU KNOW AMELIA WROTE POETRY?
I DON'T THINK I DID.
THERE'S ONE CALLED "COURAGE."
WHEN THIS IS ALL OVER REMIND ME TO TELL IT TO YOU.
I'D LIKE THAT.
BRAKKA
BRAKKA
KRAK
KRAK
SOUNDS LIKE THE BOYS HAVE GONE TO *WORK.*
BRAKKA

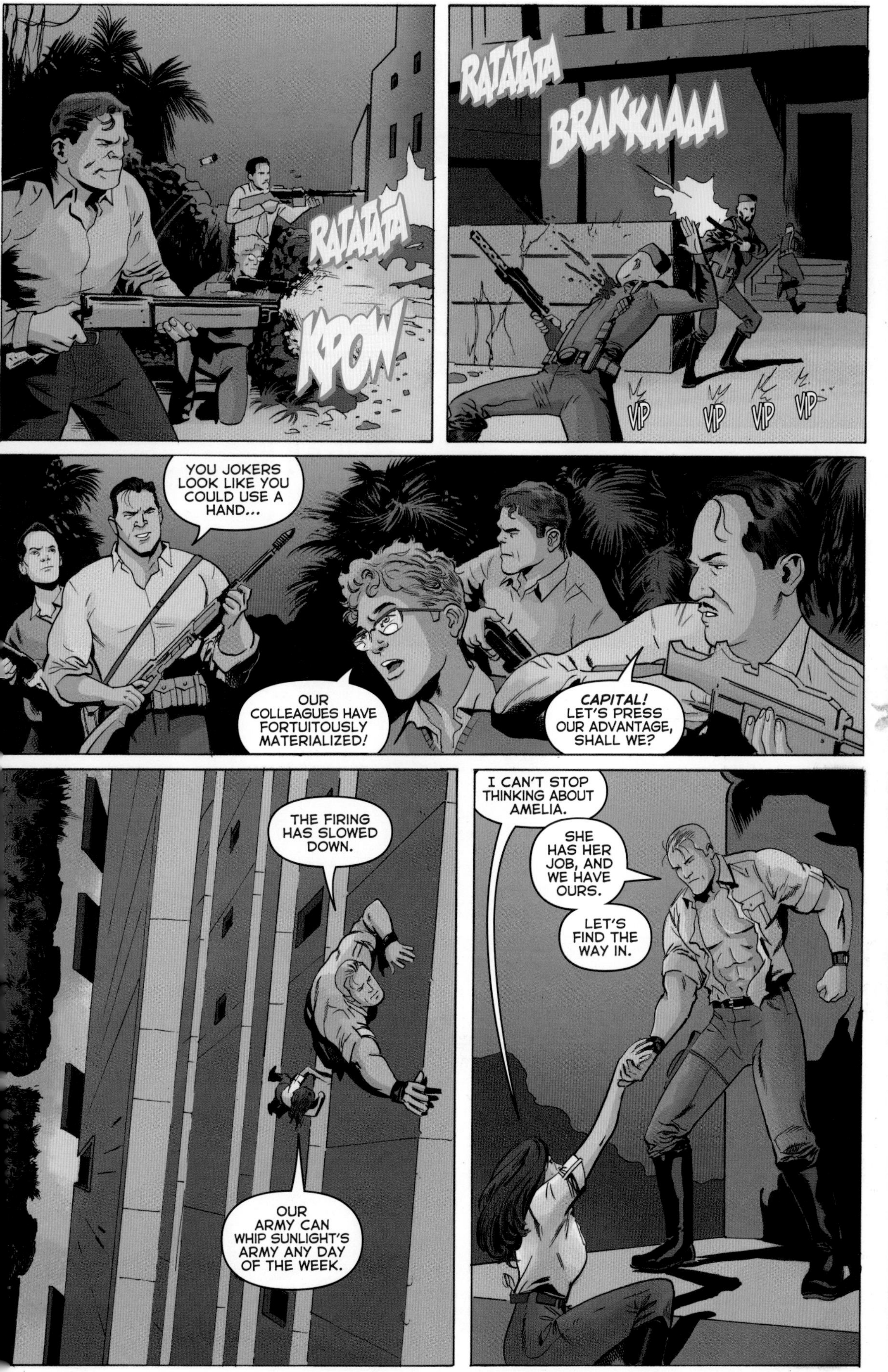
RATATATA
KPOW
RATATATA
BRAKKAAAA
VIP
VIP
VIP
VIP
YOU JOKERS LOOK LIKE YOU COULD USE A HAND...
OUR COLLEAGUES HAVE FORTUITOUSLY MATERIALIZED!
CAPITAL! LET'S PRESS OUR ADVANTAGE, SHALL WE?
THE FIRING HAS SLOWED DOWN.
OUR ARMY CAN WHIP SUNLIGHT'S ARMY ANY DAY OF THE WEEK.
I CAN'T STOP THINKING ABOUT AMELIA.
SHE HAS HER JOB, AND WE HAVE OURS.
LET'S FIND THE WAY IN.

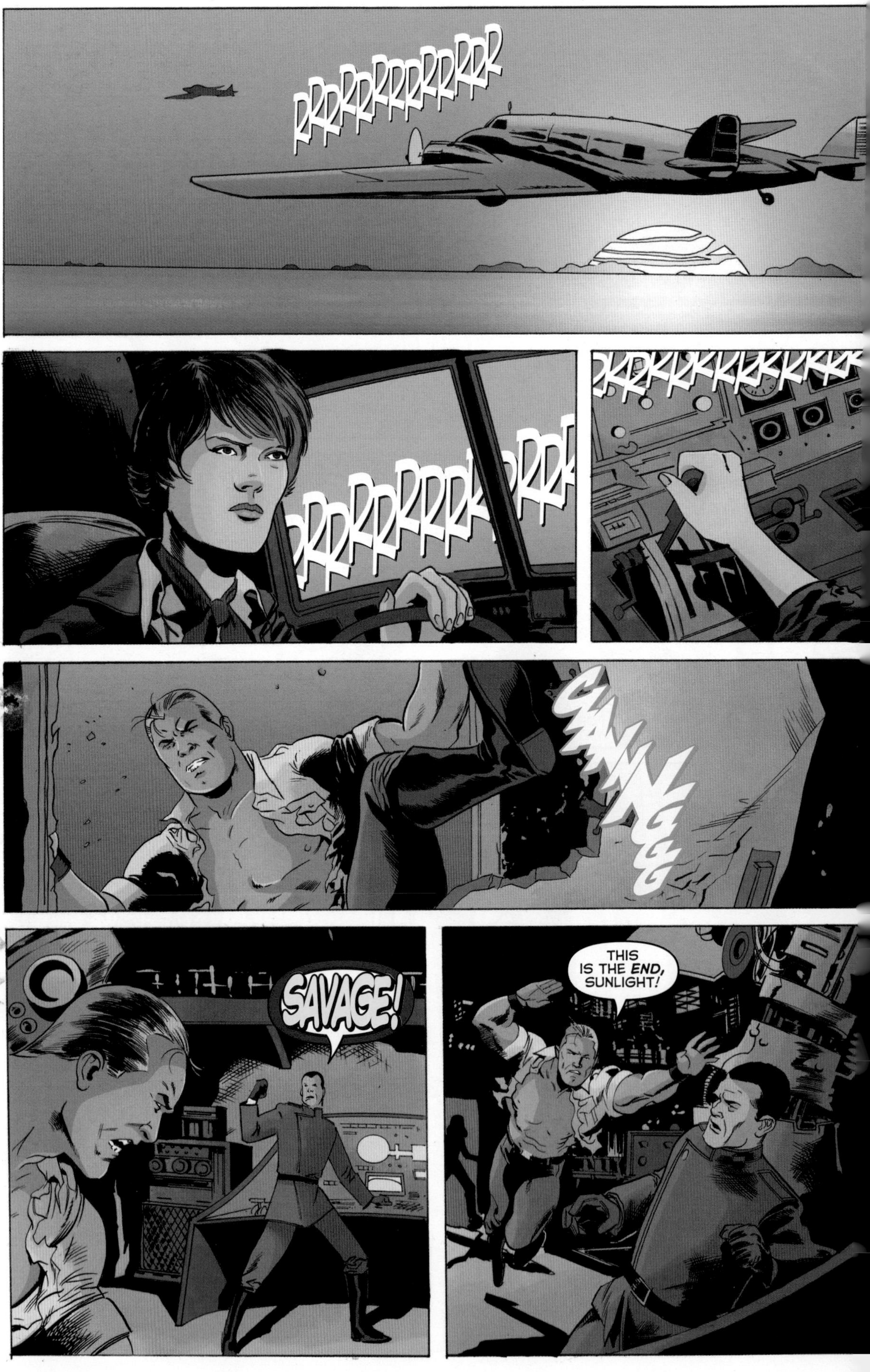
RRRRRRRRRRRRR
RRRRRRRRRRRRR
RRRRRRRRRRRRRRRRR
CLANNNGGG
SAVAGE!
THIS IS THE END, SUNLIGHT!

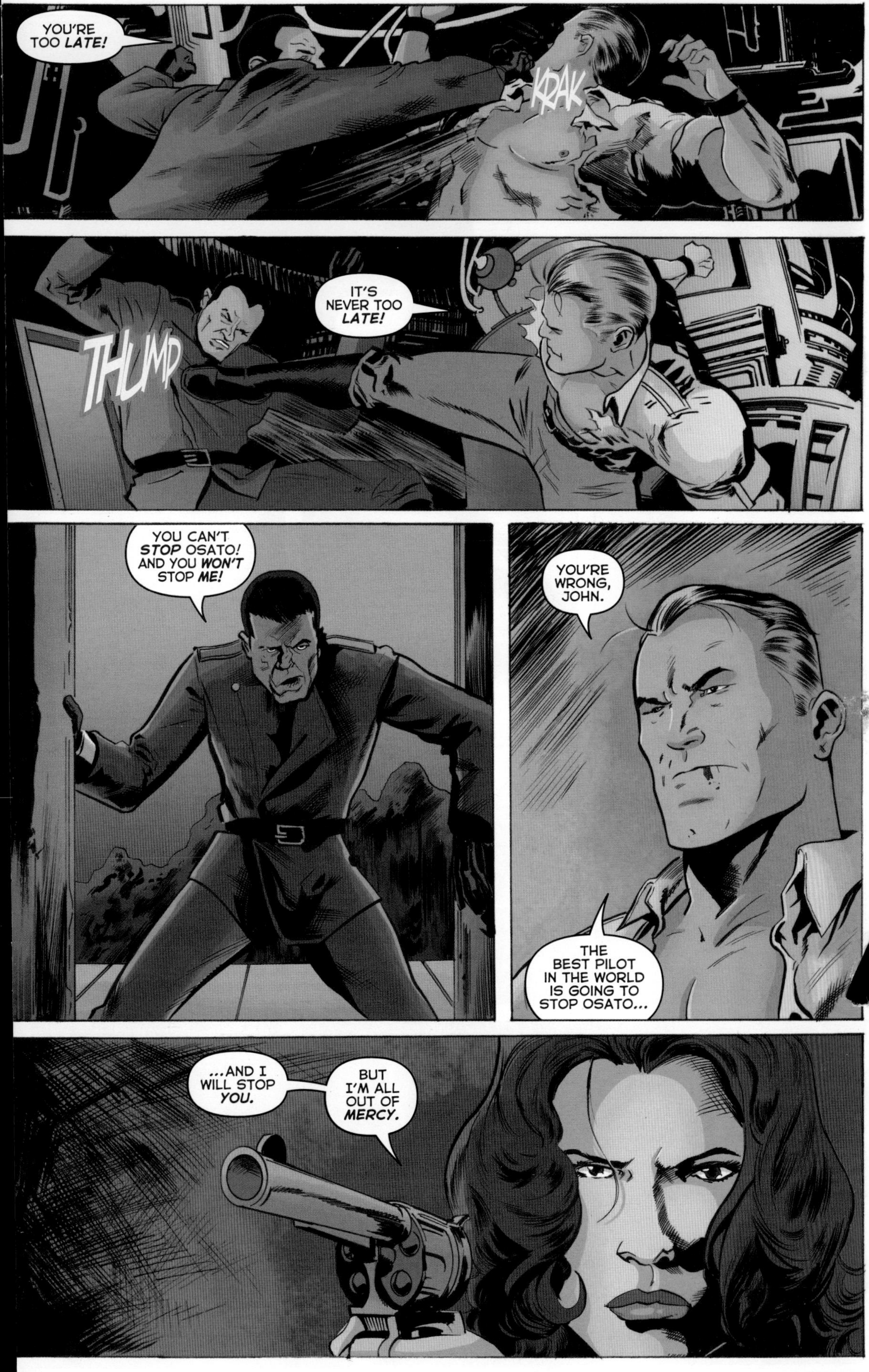
YOU'RE TOO LATE!
KRAK
IT'S NEVER TOO LATE!
THUMP
YOU CAN'T STOP OSATO! AND YOU WON'T STOP ME!
YOU'RE WRONG, JOHN.
THE BEST PILOT IN THE WORLD IS GOING TO STOP OSATO...
...AND I WILL STOP YOU.
BUT I'M ALL OUT OF MERCY.

Courage is the price that Life exacts for granting peace.

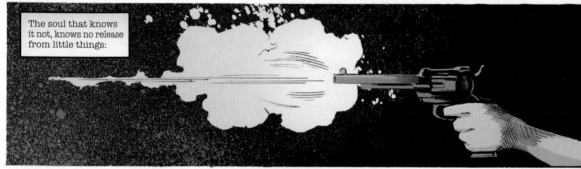

The soul that knows it not, knows no release from little things:

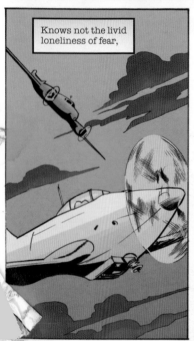

Knows not the livid loneliness of fear,

Nor mountain heights where bitter joy can hear The sound of wings.

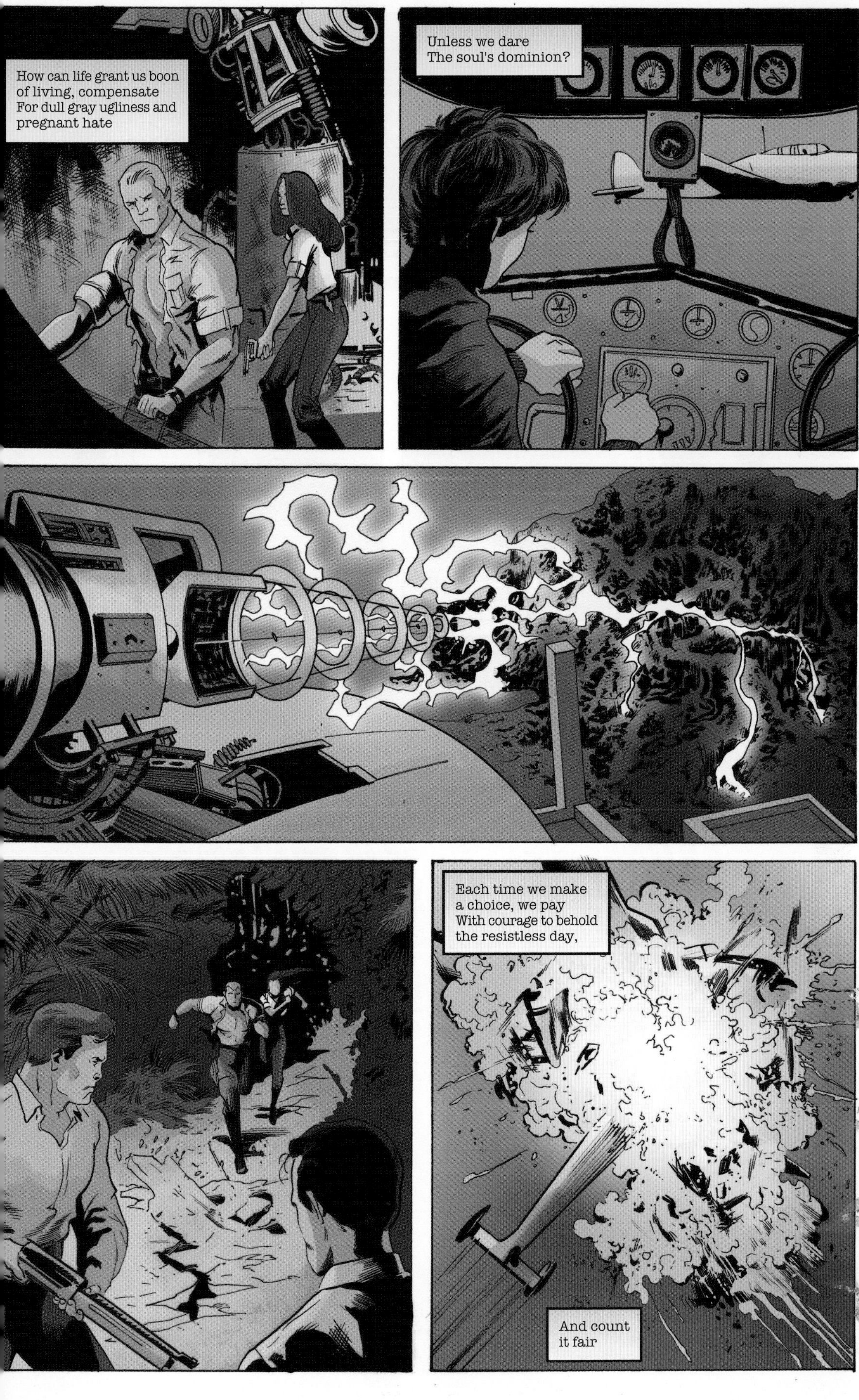
How can life grant us boon of living, compensate For dull gray ugliness and pregnant hate
Unless we dare The soul's dominion?
Each time we make a choice, we pay With courage to behold the resistless day,
And count it fair

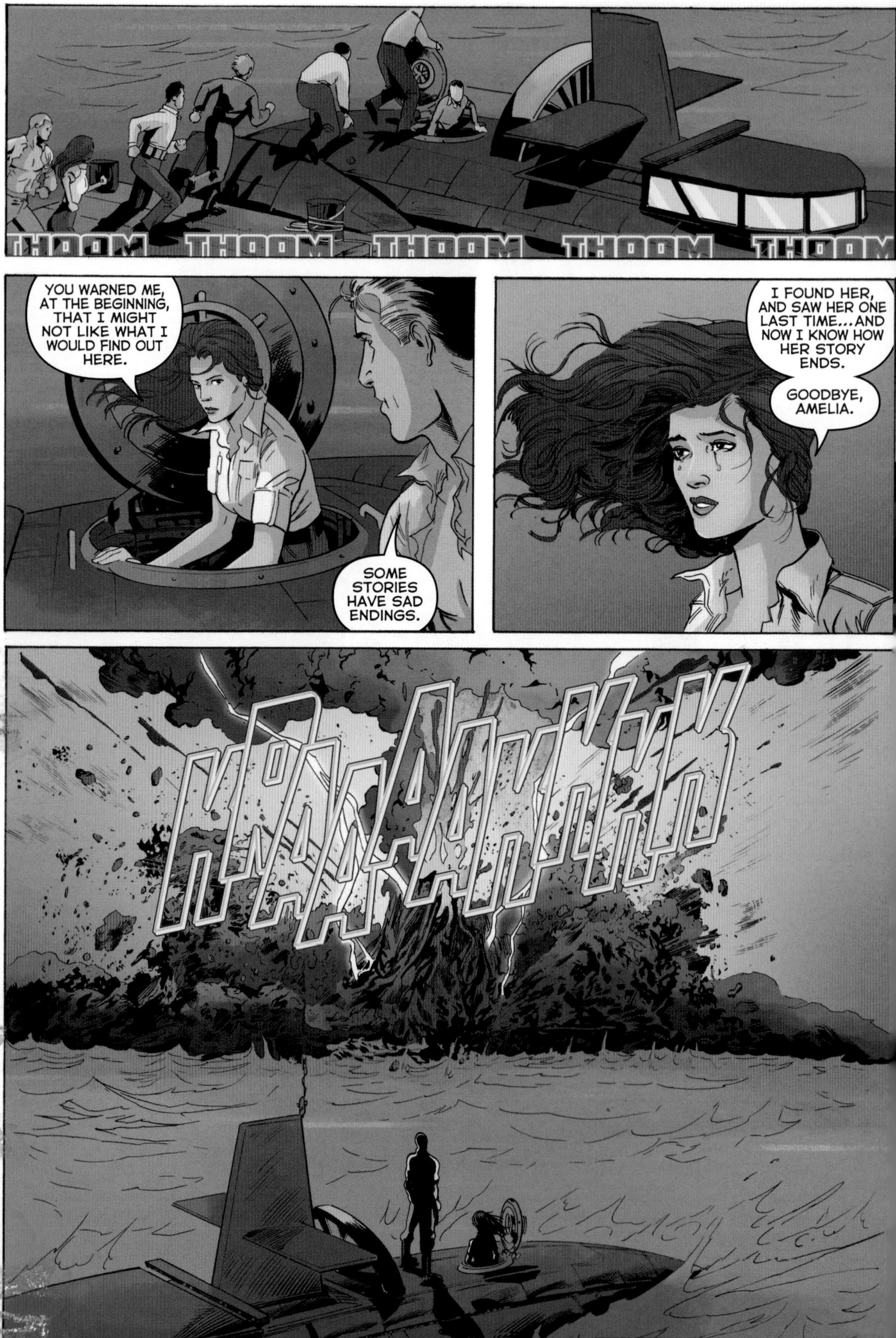
THOOM THOOM THOOM THOOM THOOM
YOU WARNED ME, AT THE BEGINNING, THAT I MIGHT NOT LIKE WHAT I WOULD FIND OUT HERE.
SOME STORIES HAVE SAD ENDINGS.
I FOUND HER, AND SAW HER ONE LAST TIME...AND NOW I KNOW HOW HER STORY ENDS.
GOODBYE, AMELIA.
KRAKAKAKAKAKOOM
THE END OF THE RING OF FIRE
BUT DOC SAVAGE WILL RETURN...

DOC SAVAGE

MONK

RENNY

Original Character Sketches
By Dave Acosta

DOC SAVAGE: THE RING OF FIRE

Afterword By David Avallone

I thought you might be interested in a little background on the making of the book you hold in your hands (or are reading on your iPad.) When Dynamite Executive Editor Joseph Rybandt kindly asked if I would be interested in doing a Doc Savage miniseries, I jumped at the chance. I love Doc, and had only done a "what-if" style Doc one-shot. I was excited to do a classic 1930s "Supersaga" in the Lester Dent tradition. Joe didn't even have to ask if I wanted my Twilight Zone: The Shadow artist back for this one... Dave Acosta and I were both looking to work together again, after having such a terrific time on that series.

To prepare for the series, Dave Acosta and I spent some time on the designs of the characters. As usual, we started a Pinterest board for visual reference. We decided on the incredibly important and controversial question of Doc's hair: a Bama-like skull-cap but one that was clearly made of real hair, which could be disturbed, and not the bizarre helmet-thing from the otherwise excellent 1970s paperback covers. We also came up with a "cast list" for the whole book, with the actors (mostly from the period) serving not as caricatures but as templates for "type". Perhaps eagle-eyed fans can figure out who was inspired by who. Or you can cheat and look up our Pinterest board for the series... Doc Savage: Ring of Photo References.

All of Anthony Marques' covers bursts with power and energy. Brent Schoonover's interconnecting covers show the path of Amelia Earhart's ill-fated round-the-world flight... a lovely touch which I didn't notice until I read something Brent wrote about it. I also didn't notice (until putting them side-by-side) that beyond the obvious use of the Bantam books font, even the formatting (the rectangle with our names and the number) mimics the great paperbacks from the 1960s/70s.

Chapter One: maybe it's a pretentious tic left over from too much Fellini, but I like opening a story with a mysterious dream sequence. We discussed a bit whether or not the audience would "get it." I felt we should give the reader the benefit of the doubt. I thought the "silence" of the scene... and Doc's horrible "death" would be enough to make the nightmare plain enough. From the very first page I loved how the book looked: the talents of Dave Acosta and colorist Morgan Hickman are very much apparent here, and on every page that followed.

I love doing the research for these period-set comics, and for what it's worth... there really was a U.S.S. Augusta, it really did carry Admiral Harry Yarnell, and there was a naval base on the Palmyra Atoll. Calling it Palmyra Island was my very weak geology "joke". It was an island before the Ring of Fire blew it in half and turned it into an atoll. I chose the Augusta because it shares a name with my beloved wife, but reading up on it I discovered it was a very significant ship in history. My favorite history teacher is honored here with the non-historical-figure Captain Calimano. Thanks, Mr. C.

Speaking of historical figures, Chapter One also has a cameo appearance by comic book hero President Franklin Delano Roosevelt, delighted to be using an early Doc Savage version of Facetime. I loved writing FDR: it's fun stuff when you have a character who – famously – really knew how to speak and express himself in interesting and charming ways. His buddy is the Secretary of the Navy, Admiral Bill Leahy. I figured Bill would be in on a call like this. This is a good place to draw your attention to the lettering of Taylor Esposito, who handled a lot of challenging stuff in the series with great imagination and talent.

Chapter Two: as the US Navy guys watch Doc Savage fall from the sky, I couldn't help myself from gently tweaking the famous superhero who owes a lot of his foundations to Doc. Doc's diving suit here can be found on the cover of the October 1937 issue of Doc Savage magazine. Old film nerds might also recognize the design of Doc Savage's gas grenades. In 1933, Doc supplied them to a filmmaker named Carl Denham, who was concerned that he might need to knock something enormous unconscious.

The issue ends with the reveal of our villain, foretold in story and song and Previews solicits: John Sunlight. I know that some fans are like "c'mon, man, John Sunlight? Again?" In prepping this series I went back and reread the Sunlight pulps and really wanted to write the character. I also felt like Kenneth Robeson/Lester Dent still left something there unfinished. Dave and I both picked the same "photo model" independently, and I love the way his design came out.

Chapter Three: Amelia at last! Her friends called her Millie. Amelia's about a decade older than Patricia Savage. Amelia spent the late twenties and early thirties giving a lot of lectures to college students, and went to a lot of events with the best and brightest young women in the country. Also... she formed an or-

PAT SAVAGE

LITTLE JOHN

HAM

Original Character Sketches
By Dave Acosta